Even Bearded Men Cried

Copyright ©2012 Brigitte Kurowski-Wilson & Bernard Marrocco

All rights reserved, including the right to reproduce this book, or a portion or portions of it, in any form whatsoever.

ISBN 978-0-9917599-2-7

Published by Marrocco Writing & Editing

www.marrocco-writing.com

Dedication

In memory of my father Johannes Speidel, my mother Ottilie, my brother Hans, my brother Walter, my sister Liselotte—all left this world too soon. — BKW

For my wife Debbie, and children Steve, Bob, Mary, Alex and Clare. — BJDM

Acknowledgements

Special thanks to Rev. Dr. Stan Chu Ilo, my friend who inspired, encouraged and believed in me. Also, thanks to my friends, and to the family of Dr. Paul and Mary Marrocco, who also gave me encouragement, and a taste of a family life. — BKW

I am most grateful to my family, without whose patience and ideas this undertaking would not have been possible. — BJDM

Table of Contents

Foreword v
1. First Things 1
2. Even Bearded Men Cried 2
3. Idyll Childhood 8
    1925 Honhardt, Germany 8
    1930 Sülzbach, Germany 8
    1934 Öhringen, Germany 16
4. Schooling 20
    1938 Öhringen, Germany 20
    1938 Ilshofen, Germany 20
    1942 Stuttgart, Germany 24
5. Education 37
    1944 Vienna, Austria 37
    1944 Wels, Austria 39
6. Consequences of War 55
    1945 Stuttgart, Germany 55
    1947 Heidenheim, Germany 64
    1949 Neuenbürg, Germany 65
    1951 Burgdorf, Switzerland 74
7. Becoming Canadian 78
    1952 Peterborough, Canada 78
8. Those Two Nice Husbands 90
    1963 Peterborough, Canada 90
    1988 Peterborough, Canada 93
9. Two Tunics to Share 96
    2003 Peterborough, Canada 96
10. Looking Back, and Ahead 101
Appendix A: Timelines of the World Wars 105
Appendix B: World War One Timeline of Johannes Speidel 106
Appendix C: Maps 107
Appendix D: Illustrations and Photographs 110

Foreword

Brigitte Kurowski-Wilson is a special person in many ways: she is a strong Catholic who incarnates some of the finest qualities of our Christian faith; she is a proud German-Canadian whose life is a narrative of the power of the human will to overcome adversity, transcend the limitations of evil and reach the mountain top by God's grace. She is a global citizen who has travelled to all the five continents of the world and who embraces people from every part of the world with so much love, affection, joy and gratitude. She is an exponent of living a healthy life style which involves daily exercise, a fitness regime, healthy eating, and a healthy spiritual and mental life. She is also a woman with a generous and kind heart who has given so much of her time and resources to helping the poor in many parts of the world, especially in Africa. Her spirit of giving has made her one of the most visible faces at the cathedral parish in Peter-borough, Canada, and in the hospital and a chiropractic clinic there. She volunteers her time and energy to the service of God, and in loving attention to the sick and the infirm.

Brigitte's life is a story worthy of reading and I am happy that she has worked with the inimitable Bernard Marrocco to put together the story of her life in very moving and fine prose.

It was Benjamin Franklin who once wrote, "If you would not be forgotten as soon as you are dead, either write something worth reading or do things worth writing." This book is not about a person's search for fame or for personal immortality; it is a story of a life well lived, but above all of a life that is guided by the mysterious hand of God. There are many heroes in the world today. Some of these make headlines, but there are millions of heroes in the world who may not make the headlines, who may not get noticed, who may never be honored, but who are touching lives in simple but profound ways. Brigitte is one of such heroes and I am sure that the story of her life will inspire many people to believe in themselves and to trust God and not lose heart.

It is only God's grace and power which can sustain a woman who lost her family in the Great Wars to hang on to the tender frame of life, to believe in the intrinsic goodness of humanity, and to step into the shadows without fearing personal annihilation. It is only God's grace which can move a frightened woman scared by wars and destruction of the best and the brightest in our humanity, to look to the darkness and choose to follow the light and move into the future without knowing where the road will lead. In the face of evil and desperation which can unnerve the human spirit and stunt human sensitivity and orientation to goodness, Brigitte emerged from the many losses in her life as a pure spirit radiating love, hope and unfailing faith.

This book is narrative of a remarkable journey; it is the story of the brokenness of our humanity, of the destructive force of violence, hatred and death. It is a story of hope in the midst of gloom and of the triumph of faith over despair, of friendship over enmity, and of light over darkness. It tells of the journey of a young woman who was touched by all the negative realities which we can ever imagine—death, loss, emptiness, violence, brokenness and betrayal. She chose not to be defined by the circumstances of her life, but to redefine her life to embrace, conquer and transcend the negative circumstances of her life.

Her story and the ups and downs of her life contained in this book give meaning to what authentic human freedom is all about. It will inspire many people through the power of God's love to bring new reality in the midst of darkness, human fragility and the all too common human dread of uncertainty and death. This book will be a guiding light to many people travelling the path of life who need a star to steady their steps and motivate them when life becomes a burden because of the unexpected tragedies of life.

Well done, Brigitte. We all thank God for giving the world a special gift through your life.

Father Stan Chu Ilo
University of St. Michael's College
Toronto, Canada
August, 2012

1. First Things

I could never ask my older brother, the one who came home with two bullets in his lung; I could never ask him questions. He was there when my father died, and I said, "Tell me," and he said, "Please, don't torture me." I said, "Who looked after us when we were by ourselves?"

I don't think he remembered very well himself. I have a feeling we had a cleaning lady, or a washing lady, who came once a month to do the washing in those days, maybe she came and fed us or took us to school or whatever. I have no idea, but he did not want to talk about any of those things.

So, I couldn't find out.

My parents died within a month of each other; my father was 48, my mother 38.

My two nieces and two nephews, that's all that I have left. They don't know anything about me, so I'll write a book about my life.

If it doesn't get published, I'll just give it to them, so they'll know.

2. Even Bearded Men Cried

My father, Johannes Speidel, was a soldier in the German Army in World War One, which began August 1, 1914. He spent only a few months in action before he was captured in September, 1914 and made a prisoner of war of the French. Although fighting ended November 11, 1918, the war was not officially over until the Treaty of Versailles was signed on June 28, 1919. Even then, some prisoners held by Allied powers were not repatriated until 1920, my father among them.

Afterward, he wrote an autobiography, which included his description of his time as a prisoner.

I knew that my father had this little book about his life, but I never saw it. First, we were only allowed to go to his library with his permission; second, he did not elaborate on his time in the war.

Over the course of World War Two, our family lost everything, including his book. All I have is this excerpt my uncle gave us, which I translated from the German.

> Captured in battle in the Argonne in September, 1914. Totally exhausted, followed by an eight day and night transport in a rail car, from Bar-le-Duc to Castres in the Tarn department. Traveled without any food. We ate what the guards discarded, which caused us diarrhea with blood.
>
> In Castres we were brought to a citadel-like cloister; the cells faced the courtyard, and were completely isolated, bare of any furnishings. We slept on the floor on smelly thin straw, exactly like sardines in a can.
>
> There was one tiny window, and at sunrise everybody tried to get near the window to get a little warmth. Everyone was cold and hungry.
>
> Twice a day we got watery soup, sometimes with a few pieces of potato, and 400 grams of bread. If I moved, I got dizzy.
>
> Those who knew a trade were sent to work in the town. The intellectuals had to work with picks and shovels.
>
> A variety of insects prevented us from sleeping. The rats came in at night through the tiny window, which had only one iron rod across it.
>
> After three months we received some soap, and I got a second shirt.
>
> During my entire 5-1/2 years as a prisoner of war, I stole a half-liter of milk. It was the only time we saw any milk. The coffee was made from figs, and tasted terrible.
>
> After four months, in February 1915, transported to Cordes. This was the most romantic place I had seen so far. A fortress in the old Spanish style; so beautiful from the distance, like a fairy tale. The fortress on the hill gave an incomparable impression. It looked beautiful in the sunshine and the moonshine.
>
> For me as an intellectual, I had to work again with picks and shovels. But there was an improvement. Again our quarters were in a cloister, sleeping on straw. We daily had black beans, with an occasional piece of horsemeat in the soup (which tasted horrible), and 800 grams of bread.
>
> There, the foolish insistence of my German comrades to show the French what a

German can do led to revengeful consequences. Everybody was ordered to work harder, under the watchful eyes of the guards; I was close to exhaustion. Even bearded men cried.[1]

I got pneumonia with high fever, and I was arrested because I insulted the French doctor with my remark, "*Grande nation.*"[2] I also developed bronchitis, but had to continue to work, until someone took pity on me, and granted me eight days of rest.

Again from five in the morning to eight at night, digging endlessly.

My friend Stein saved me from dying of hunger. He gave me one piece of bread with some kind of fat. With this alone he earned himself a place in heaven—it proves to me with great satisfaction, joy and admiration, that his spirituality had not faltered in his suffering in that cruel prison.

The two of us tried to organize a strike. Of 60 comrades, three men were detained: Speidel, Stein his friend and a third man. All three were arrested, and taken in a wooden truck to a dirty cell. It was between two toilets and the kitchen, and had no window. Facing south, the heat was unbearable, along with the foul odor.

On the second day, we had not received any bread or water. I was overcome by an uncontrollable anger and swung myself, with the last of my strength, against the door. The guard came with a stick; if he would have touched me, I would have fought back. After that we got some water and bread.

From the roof, our comrades installed a sort of elevator, to send some food down in a basket, which we could reach through a tiny gap in the wall.

A few days later, the French guards were shooting it down, from the window opposite. Five more prisoners were added to our small cell. Half-conscious from exhaustion, we endured 15 days on the bare floor, without any cover. Another prisoner, from Bavaria, slept for eight days, uninterrupted. There was just one bucket for a toilet, which could only be emptied every few days. We pressed ourselves to the window to get some fresh air.

One day the door opened, and a new prison commandant appeared, and introduced himself as *fortes têtes*[3].

I refused to work on Good Friday, and had to spend Easter in a cell.

Soon afterward I was assigned to work at a quarry. I could not conceal a smile toward the owner's mistress. Again into a cell for three nights, without any food at all.

I also was charged for a strike and protesting, which gave me eight more days in a cell.

Again, the Germans wanted to show the French what a German worker can do. I, the

---

[1] The original German: Ja sogar bärtige Männer weinten.
[2] An idiom used by Germans to deprecatingly mock France and the French as being self-important.
[3] Stubborn, hard-headed.

teacher, had to keep up—I could not do less.

Soon I had an accident. Two very heavy rocks fell on my toes, and blood ran out over my high boots. I was transported in a wheel barrow to the prison hospital at Cordes for four weeks.

Soon after my release, I went on strike. I felt too weak to work. Arrested, and sent back to the unpopular but familiar prison in Castres.

The year was 1916.

At Augmontel and Mazamet in the Cevennes, in the forest detachment. My boots were in shreds, yet I had to work in this wet forest of the Montagne Noire (Black Mountain). The result was catastrophic.

Bloody diarrhea, which did not get any better, plus a toothache, one as I had never experienced in my life before. This lasted for four months. I rolled on the floor with pain, which made me weak and exhausted. Nobody cared for me, because I was considered dangerous. I was tossed into a camp in Montauban on the Garonne River, with very little food. I was near starvation.

In July, 1916, we were sent to the Romane prison in the Drôme department. The trip took us past the Pyrenees through the Rhône valley to Valence, where we were greeted by the people at the railway station with oranges, dirt and stones. Three days later we arrived in Romane[4], and from there to Lyon.

On the Rhône River in the commune of Villeurbanne, quite near Lyon, I became a construction worker. We had to build a radio station. We had to carry the mortar on our backs, 15 meters up. Far away in the east glittered Mont Blanc. To the south there was a beautiful church, on a hill on the other side of the Rhône.

We received daily potato soup with smelly tripe. I developed bleeding abscesses, and my weight went down to 80 pounds.

A nice French doctor treated me three times, and he confirmed, "*Vous vous faites du mauvais sang.*"[5]

I went on strike, and I was sent back to the notorious prison camp, Romane, for the second time.

Our diet was goat cheese infested with worms. I approached the commander about it, and was declared to be a rebel.

In the spring of 1917, moved on to Séchilienne, near Grenoble in the French Alps.

There we had to dig a channel, and falling rocks crashed onto my toes. The high altitude of the mountains raised my blood pressure, and I also suffered from headaches from the warm wind from the south (in German, *Föhnwind*).

---

[4] Likely Romans-sur-Isère.
[5] A French idiom meaning 'You worry too much' (literally—your blood is not healthy).

In April, my friend Weiler and I decided to escape. We lived on the first floor of a shed-like house. A ladder in the backyard connected with a cage housing pigeons. One night at 1 AM, we climbed down a rope. I was barefoot, and landed on broken glass. The sole of my foot was badly cut, and we had no choice other than surrender. Four weeks under strict observation in the prison in La Mure was our punishment— just bread and water, relieved only every fourth day by a warm soup.

I was discharged from the prison and sent to several farmers. I had to sleep in a filthy barn on filthy hay with 25 comrades for 30 days. Promptly at midnight every night we were ordered to empty the public toilets, which took us until 4 AM.

A few days later, we were transported south, to Ribiers near Sisteron. For the first time in three years, I felt like a human being again. I worked for a farmer, helping with the harvest: fresh clothes, proper meals, I thought I was in heaven. I was ordered to help another farmer, where it was even better, but with the first snowfall all had ended.

Transported to La Bâtie-Neuve near Gap. I felt that I was condemned from paradise. I had to stand in a sewer in December, a cold wind blowing from the surrounding mountains and glaciers. Another comrade and I decided to strike in that terrible cold temperature. We lived in a coal cellar without windows. The cold and no food brought us to hopeless despair. I made the guards deliberately angry, to get out of there.

Transferred to a prison at Gap, and afterward to Marseille.

The device in this camp was hunger. I had to work in a petroleum plant at the harbor, and after that on a railroad at Sainte-Tulle. I refused to dig in the ditch. Arrested and imprisoned for three days in a baking oven of a cell.

Transferred again; sheep herding. Three days later by telegraphic order, sent to a military camp at Carpiagne near Marseille, working the entire day clearing the area. The food was atrocious. The bread tasted like it had been made with sawdust. I was so hungry, sleeping was impossible. I became so desperate, I looked for an exit, a way to escape.

Luckily, I was suddenly transferred to Paris. Unfortunately, the city was under artillery fire and attacks from German planes.

Again on the move, this time to Étampes, between Paris and Orleans, constructing an airport for the Americans. We received black beans from South America daily, infested with insects, and twice per week we were given stale bread.

With the next transport I landed in Rouen, in another prison camp: work at the harbor, for eight weeks. Our food was rice cooked in water, and potatoes instead of bread. There were 2,000 of us. We all became thieves, stealing what we could: English cigarettes, brandy, sardines, cheese, coal, sugar, salt, bread, coffee, clothes, laundry. Everything went with us.

I experienced some humorous incidents. If someone got caught, he went either to the jail or before a war tribunal.

Several times I have been the guest of five different prisons.

December 1918—in another camp, at Croisset near Rouen. Here there was a fracas between the Kaiser's sympathizers and the German republicans. As a republican, I was separated and sent to Dieppe. I was assigned to work at the harbor, handling steel. It was the worst of the worst camps, and known for starvation. I refused immediately, was arrested and sent for 15 days to Dunkirk, three of the days without any food. One comrade died of starvation.

Everybody stole whatever we could find, including hundreds of wine barrels. We found bacon and ate it raw. One comrade was shot to death by a drunken French soldier.

I became a translator, and was assigned to an office to sort out parcels. I had two helpers, both of whom chose to escape. I was ordered to give any information, but refused.

I was sent with my regiment by train to La Madeleine, near Lille. A collision occurred on the way. I was able to jump out of the speeding train, but many died or were injured.

In La Madeleine there were lots of repairs to be done. Six sergeants were bribed by a French man to get us to work for him. Two other comrades and I went on strike, but somebody betrayed us, and all three were sent to separate camps. One of my comrades, from East Prussia, died; I never heard what became of the second one. I was the third one, who survived.

I arrived in Anor, near Fourmies. There we had to blow up damaged ammunition. The food consisted of rice and potatoes, alternately. One got allergic to rice, and I could not eat it any more.

Millions of grenades were blown up, together with 11 comrades. Death lurked around us. Many times we had to escape in a hurry. We also inhaled several kinds of poisonous gases.

One day, the whole ammunition dump exploded, and gas filled the air, which irritated our eyes. We cried for many hours.

The last transport brought us to Olnoi[6], on the Sambre River. It was December, 1919. Again, I refused to work. My punishment was 30 days in a wet cellar, with neither bread nor soup. It was the favorite French revenge, to refuse bread to a prisoner. I spent Christmas, and New Year's 1920, in that cellar.

My release from Hell was on February 24, 1920. Four days later, I arrived home in Heilbronn, Germany.

---

[6] In French, Aulnoye.

A broken man! Thus ended a senseless tragedy, with traumatic consequences. It robbed my siblings and me of fully knowing our wonderful father and hero.

I was just a child when I heard for the first time from my father that he had been a prisoner. He hadn't divulged much about it, and he never actually really talked about it — maybe because I was too young, or maybe because I didn't know what to ask. But I knew that he was in a prisoner of war camp.

He said it was a better France now than when he was there. I said how much I hated the French for what they had done to him, but he said, "No, no, no, don't you hate them. You don't even know anything about them. Don't hate anybody. In a war, people do things which they may not be responsible for." Therefore, I never hated anybody.

I cried when I first read this excerpt. If only I'd had a chance to talk with my father about it when I was older. There would have been so many questions: Why was he so forgiving? Why didn't he hate them? What gave him the strength and stamina to survive?

I don't know why my father rebelled so much when he was a prisoner. That's another question I would have liked to have asked him. He didn't want to give in, although he was arrested and re-arrested.

3. Idyll Childhood

1925 Honhardt, Germany

I was born on the 21st of September, 1925, in Honhardt, near Stuttgart in Germany. It was a Monday. My new name was Brigitte Speidel, though I didn't receive a middle name. I was the third child in our family, with two brothers ahead of me, and one sister after.

The time of day I was born, I don't know. Whether it was a house or a hospital, I don't know. I was too young to ever ask my parents any of those questions.

1930 Sülzbach, Germany

Home

I must have been four or five years old when my father, a school teacher, transferred to a new location. It was in a small place called Sülzbach, a village really. It wasn't far from my father's home town of Heilbronn, which is on the Neckar River.

We lived next to our church there, *Kilianskirche* (St. Kilian's), which was Protestant—I was Lutheran before. My father was the organist. My father's father also played organ in his church in Heilbronn, for 30 years without missing a Sunday. He made his own compositions, too. (My brother had copies, but I don't know what happened to them during the war.)

We lived on top of the schoolhouse, in an apartment on the fourth floor. The school was on top of a hill, and the minister lived opposite in the *Pfarrhaus* (parsonage), beside the church. The church was surrounded by a big stone wall—this was our playground. There were a lot of pine trees and fruit trees, and all the parishioners could come and pick the fruit. There was even a little garden where you could plant vegetables.

Before I was old enough to go to school, my mother would send me downstairs and I could sit with the first grade girls, and listen to them. I could spend some time in the classroom, although I had to be quiet—if I got restless, my father would tell me to leave. Later, when I started school myself, I could already count. I knew some things, because I had already been listening to them. I learned the ABCs early.

It was a happy childhood. When we lived in Sülzbach, once I was old enough to join in, I played together with my brothers. We all enjoyed ourselves.

We had a wonderful time in the church playground there—it was enough for us, that playground. We acted out plays. My brothers built us an underground sort of a cave, and covered it up with wooden planks, and then leaves and grass and moss on top. We had our meetings, underground there. We had an old telephone in it, although it didn't work.

We played Indians in our underground lair, too. We knew about Indians because we read Karl May books—we had a big library, and we were always reading books. Karl May was a famous German writer, and he wrote all about the American Indians. He must have studied in America, because he knew an awful lot about Indians. My brothers read them, and I read them, too.

My brother Walter, two years older than me, was the Indian chief. My grandmother, for some reason, had gotten him an Indian headdress, complete with feathers. I was the lookout. If the enemy was sighted, I was supposed to ring a bell (using the old telephone). I would pretend we were being attacked. The attackers would be the minister's children from across the street. We were allowed to play only with them, and only inside the compound of the churchyard.

Walter raised rabbits, and my older brother Hans (four years older than me) liked cats[1]. So we had a cat. That cat came every morning to the boys' bedroom, and meowed, and woke them up. The cat knew what time we had to go to school. Except on Sundays; somehow, the cat knew that on Sunday it didn't need to come.

I liked playing with my brothers. My brother Walter whistled, but my mother did not allow me to whistle. She said it was not ladylike. But I learned to whistle anyway. We children communicated by whistling (even though I wasn't allowed to do that!).

Hans liked to knit, and he joined in with the neighborhood girls to work on it.

Since my playmates were mostly my brothers, when they started to play with a sling for firing stones, of course I tried it too. Unfortunately I hit the pastor in the back. This was the end of the sling, with a stern warning from my father. (Oh, how hard it was to face the pastor, and to apologize.)

I always wanted to wear my hair in braids, just like the other girls at that time. After it grew as long as down to my shoulders, my brothers decided that they preferred me with bangs and short hair. They found some scissors, and off it came. Another time, I had a loose baby tooth; mischievous as boys are, Hans and Walter put a string around it, and pulled.

My brothers sometimes used me for their own purposes. It used to be the fashion that at Easter and Christmas they had a separate service at church for the children, and afterward we got candy in the shape of Easter bunnies. The candy was hidden around the garden, chocolate rabbits or sugar eggs, and we had to go and look for it. It was a gift for the children, for after the Easter church service. Some children in our *Kirchspiel* (parish) didn't attend that particular Easter Sunday, because their families were away. But their candy was saved in the sacristy for the following Sunday. We were allowed to play only with the minister's children, if you'll remember, and he had two boys and a girl, or maybe one boy and a girl. The following Saturday, the sacristan, or caretaker, was cleaning the church, and the windows were left open. There were iron grates over the windows, but we could see through them, and we saw the table with the chocolates and all the things that had been left there for the children. My brothers got the idea for me to sneak in, timed for when the caretaker would be at the front of the church. I was to go in behind the sacristy and then come out to distribute all the candy. So this is what I did. Together with the minister's children, we went down to our special underground place and ate happily. We enjoyed it.

That evening, when we were at supper, we heard steps coming up the stairs. The caretaker had arrived, and we knew right away: "Oh, oh," we thought. Having just come from the minister, he told our parents about all the things have been taken and eaten—the minister's children had said we did it. So my father said, "Come here." We finally confessed: that I had gone in there, and that it was everybody's idea in a way. He said, "Wash your hands, clean your teeth and go to bed." We had to stop eating, we couldn't finish our supper and we had to go to bed. That night he didn't come to say 'Good night' to us, and we were so unhappy. Very bad. I went over to my brothers' room, and we cried.

The next day, we were called over to the minister's office. The minister told us, "You know what you did. It's stealing, and stealing is a sin." Then he was telling us about Noah's Ark, and he said that all the sinners were drowned, and they never got on the ark—only the good people did. He said that was what would happen to us.

---

[1] When Hans at age 14 heard from my father that we were blessed with another sister, he proclaimed that he would rather have seven cats instead! Later, after we moved to Ilshofen, it was he who took my sister to a lovely playground, and sat on a bench studying while watching her play in the sandbox.

After that, we sat together and prayed that if there was a flood[2], we wouldn't get swept away by it. After five or six days, my older brother—I was five or six, he must have been nine or ten—he said to us, "Just think, we live up on a hill. Since when does water ever run up a hill?" "Yes, that's right," we agreed. So we gave up praying to avoid floods. But we learned our lesson. For the first time in my life I realized what stealing was.

In the evenings, we children had our sedentary time, before we went to bed. We had to read, and we had to learn how to write letters. Thank-you letters to our godparents, for example—when they sent us something for Christmas, our parents made us sit down and write letters.

The books I read were chosen by my parents. *Heidi* was a favorite one. I read my brothers' books, too. Sherlock Holmes (in German!). Karl May's books.

My father was fluent in German and French. We spoke German at home. He played the piano and violin and flute and organ. My mother took singing lessons.

There were no money problems for our family. My mother, Ottilie Speidel, had inherited some from her mother, Lena Günther. We children got pocket money. Anything we wanted, we could have. However, money was not discussed.

We had a maid for nine years; Rosa was her name. She lived with us, and was with us almost all the time, although she had Sundays off. In those days, you did a big washing once a month; it was a two-day affair for the maid. In the evenings, she sat with us. She got married six months before my mother died. We had to respect the maid. We did what she said. We helped her every day, such as with drying dishes. My brothers were careful, even counting the forks, to make sure the work was divided evenly.

Christmas

Christmases were wonderful, even though we never saw a Christmas tree until Christmas Eve. In most European countries, Christmas Eve is the main part of Christmas, when you open your gifts. My father took us to the theater in the afternoon of Christmas Eve, a children's theater, from something like two to four o'clock. I saw *The Nutcracker* (many times), *Hansel and Gretel* and all kinds of little shows. We were always taken to the theater. While we were there, my mother and the maid set up everything for Christmas.

The Christmas tree we never saw until evening. The trees were blue spruce, so there were no branches immediately above that could catch fire, and there were real candles and decorations (glass bulbs). I never helped set up the Christmas tree, because we were always away while it went up, and we were not allowed to touch it afterward.

Our special toys that we saw only at Christmas would have been brought out. I had a dollhouse, with miniature furniture, a grocery store, and an electric stove with two three-inch diameter heating pads. My brothers had a real railroad, a castle with soldiers and a steam contraption with a whistle. All of them were set up in the living room, and there were new gifts under the tree. When we came back from the theater (we were already festively dressed up), we were not allowed to go into the living room yet. After a while, we heard a little bell ringing. That meant *Sankt Nikolaus* (Saint Nicholas/Santa Claus) and the Christ Child just left, after having gotten everything ready for us. Then we were allowed into the room, and there was no light on except the candles. My father sat at the piano and played Christmas songs, and my mother sang. *Stille Nacht* (Silent Night) was always last. Then we were allowed to play with the toys for a while, and then came supper.

A nice custom was that that the toy railroads could be as long as a room. They weren't cheap, they were metal, aluminum or something like that, and the rail lines (tracks) fit into

---

[2] There was a river nearby called the Sulm, a tributary of the Neckar, which overflowed sometimes.

one another. The railroad was manufactured by the famous Märklin Company, which is still doing it today. There were other recreational playthings for my brothers, such as Walter's construction set with real metal screws and bolts. He enjoyed building bridges.

The castle, and the soldiers, and my dollhouse were all handmade. Despite their grandeur, after a while, say by January or February, we lost interest. My parents asked if it would be all right if *Sankt Nikolaus* could come and pick it all up and store it away for next Christmas. "Yes," we would say. It was stored away, and since it wasn't lying around, it wasn't destroyed—it was a good way of preserving it, rather than having it just gather dust and end up broken. Every year, just like the Christmas tree, the toys were new again, because you forgot. Every year, we had the same toys. We got new gifts as well, but those big things were always eventually stored away.

The gifts we got were typically things to wear, jewelry, books and things like that.

After supper came *Sankt Nikolaus* (my parents hired a friend to play this part). He had a sack with him. He always had a special gift in there for each of us. One year, my father had said to us, "Do you have a wish for something? Which architecture do you like?" I was particular to Italian architecture and my brother Walter preferred French architecture. So we got big books about architecture, about the buildings in those countries. *Sankt Nikolaus* gave us the gifts, but not before saying something like, "You were bad. You did this. You did this. You did that." He knew everything we did, and he made us promise not to do it again, and then he gave us the special gift.

I believed it was really *Sankt Nikolaus* for a while, until one year my mother was in the hospital, and my brother Hans said, "It's a miserable Christmas. I don't even enjoy it any more. Our mother is not here, and there is no *Sankt Nikolaus*."

It was the only time of the year where we could stay up and play as long as we wanted, even after my parents had gone to bed.

Next day, Christmas, we went to church, and of course my father played the organ. Afterward, we either had company, or we were invited out. Christmas Day was strictly for visiting. When company came, like my uncles, they all disappeared into the music room, and played—the piano, four-handed, and one played the violin. There was music all the time at our house. People used to say (in the summer), "If you don't know where Mr. Speidel lives, the windows are always open, just go by the music; listen for and hear the music."

When the time for the Christmas tree being indoors was done, we'd take it out to the garden and play Christmas all over again.

On *Karfreitag* (Good Friday), we weren't allowed to play—there was no such thing as playing on the street on that day. (On Sundays, you were not allowed to go out there, either.) I hated Good Friday because you were not allowed to even go out. "Good Friday," my parents said, "was when Christ died, and you'll stay here. You're going to read or something like that; this is not the time for fooling around."

My parents were really observant, good Christians. They observed the majesty of God. You behaved yourself in church. You dressed up for church. You had respect for church.

They helped people, and were good to people. They cooked food for the unemployed (there was bad unemployment before Adolf Hitler came to power). We had fruit trees—we had grapes, we had apples, we had pears, we had plums—it was all ours, but my parents said to the people, "Please come and help yourselves." They were helping others, and it was obvious to me as a child that they did so. However, I didn't recognize it as Christianity as such; it was just what everybody did.

We prayed. I had to pray every day. I prayed every night, before I went to bed. I prayed at noontime, before the main meal of the day, "*Vater, segne diese Speise uns zur Kraft und dir zum Preise. Amen.*" (Father, bless this food for your praise and for our strength.)

My Parents

My mother was like me, and I was like her. She was friendly, she talked to everybody. She was respected; I could tell that she was respected. She liked the theater. She liked music. People always talked to her. As a child you don't observe that much, but I wish I would have been more alert, or more aware of it. You wake up afterward. There are so many questions I wanted to ask my mother, afterward. For example, I don't know whether I had measles or not. I did have diphtheria, I know that. Nowadays, twelve-year olds know a lot, but it wasn't like that then.

I looked a little bit more like my grandmother than my mother. My mother had a full head of auburn-brown hair, like me. I think she had brown eyes.

She helped with the household, with the maid. She had tea parties in the afternoon sometimes, when she invited friends. She had singing lessons. I think she played the piano, but I'm not sure.

When she went somewhere with us, she would have pictures taken. She had an album made up for each of us, with the same photographs. She made us read, and when we got gifts she made us sit down and write thank-you letters. She was a good mother, but she was so sick so many times.

She had fun. She had a sense of humor, although you don't notice that so much when you're a small child. She went on trips with the other teachers. One time one of her friends had her hat blown off, and there was a picture of my mother laughing as she chased the hat for her. She laughed, and laughed and laughed.

My parents went dancing, and they went to the opera in Heilbronn when we were in Sülzbach.

I don't know how my parents met. I wish I did. A train trip from Ilshofen, where she grew up, to Heilbronn, where my father grew up, might have taken 45 minutes or so. I know my mother took singing lessons at one time or another, and that my father was a musician—there might have been some connection there. As a wedding gift, my maternal grandmother gave my parents a house. When they came back from their honeymoon, everything was in it—furniture, even food in the kitchen. I don't think my father ever taught in Heilbronn. There's nobody alive who knows. My older brother would never talk about these things. "Please, please," he would say, "never even mention the past."

My parents had principles, and we knew what was expected of us. We had to do it, and if not, well, there's no other way. For example, if I wanted something and my father said no, then I went to my mother. She'd ask if I'd talked to father, and I said yes, and then she asked what he said. I'd tell her, and she'd say, "OK, that's it. No." They had their rules, they had discipline. We had our playtime, we could be happy. If we were getting out of hand, misbehaving, they only had to look at us.

She was a disciplinarian, just like my father. Neither interfered with the other. If I went to my father, he would ask what she said, and he would say that was the way it was. They went together to church, and we had to behave. There were traditions and etiquette to follow, and she always made sure we obeyed. If I had to deliver a message from my father to a colleague, if I had to go to their house, it would always be between 11 o'clock and 12, though you didn't stay long—maybe half an hour, and then you'd leave. You would wait until you'd been asked to sit—you didn't just sit. When I went somewhere, she would tell me to be careful and not bump into any furniture (which I was known to sometimes accidentally do), and to be polite. There were many such imperatives.

My mother was reserved. She was a good mother to us. She did what every mother does: she loved us. I didn't like *Spinat* (spinach), and my mother didn't give in when I didn't want to eat it. She was determined that I not win that battle, and I had to eat that spinach, even it was cold two hours later.

They showed us their love for us in daily things by hugging, and sitting in the lap, and kissing, and putting their arm around me, and saying "Come with me."

My father lost a lot of umbrellas, so before he went out of the house she would say, "Have you got your umbrella? Have you got your wallet? Have you got your money?"

When my father was still healthy, he played the organ; he conducted the men's choir, and went to choir competitions in other towns. He loved the theater. He played the piano, every minute that he had the time. He painted. On Sundays, we'd go somewhere, and we'd pick flowers, and then he would paint them using oil paints. I remember being with him in the countryside, and him having his palette in his hand. We were standing up on a hill, and there was this little village, and they were hanging their featherbed mattresses out the windows for the sun. There were storks on the roofs of the village. I remember him with the palette in his hand, and with his pencil and brush. He took measurements with his brush, looking into the distance.

Vater (Father) was fun. He was good in telling stories, and inventing stories. He taught singing. We had to do singing, too.

My father was a good swimmer. I remember him taking us to an outdoor pool in Heilbronn on the river Neckar, and me sliding down the water slide, and my father catching me and giving me a ride on his back.

He was a well-respected person. I was over there in Germany many years later for a visit, and I met a man in Sülzbach who had been a pupil of my father's, and he said, "You know, your father was respected outside the school. If something happened, we said, 'Just wait. We'll tell Mr. Speidel tomorrow.'"

One year the maid was doing housecleaning. The stairs from the school up to our living quarters were carpeted. It was held down with brass rods, which once a year were lifted and taken out to be cleaned. We had a maid at that time, and she used a carpet beater. Since it was a long carpet, all the school children were holding it, side-by-side, and she was knocking the dust off with the beater. We were all fed chocolates afterward.

My father had some kind of a container on his desk, and if a student was late for school, they would have to put in a small coin. This accumulated throughout the year, whereupon my father would add whatever money was needed to cover the cost of a bus trip somewhere interesting, typically into a nearby forest. (With the beautiful surroundings in Europe, you don't have to go far, even within Germany.) There were hiking trails, so you could never get lost. My father would divide us into two groups, with a leader for each. He would walk away and hide in the woods. Whichever group found him first got chocolate. That was part of the entertainment for the walk, to make it fun. He might lie in a ditch covered up with leaves. I was always annoyed if the other group found him first, and they got the chocolate. (He never put me in as a leader, naturally.) That was fun.

The chocolate would often be a kind that had crisped rice on the bottom, covered in milk chocolate. In those days, dark chocolate wasn't so popular, like it is now.

During cold weather, he'd sometimes ask, "Do you want to go out for recess, or do you want to stay in?" We'd say, "Yes, we want to stay, and we want you to tell us a fairy tale." He was an appealing and accomplished story teller, particularly in the way he added his own ideas and imagination. One favorite story was about Kalif the Stork. He was an Arabian prince who had been turned into a stork because he had been bad. He had to stay a stork until a princess came along and kissed him, which would turn him back into a prince again. Oh, my, the way he described the princess, and how sad the stork was as he stood up in a tower of the castle overlooking the valley—such a joy for a child to listen to. We always asked him to tell us fairy tales.

I was then old enough to enjoy his piano playing at home. Any free time he had, he went to play the piano. If any relative came, an uncle or a cousin, they disappeared into the music room to play together. Sometimes he would accompany them on the violin, or sometimes they would play four-hand piano. His favorite composers were Chopin and Beethoven. He played everyone else, of course, and played the organ as well as the flute.

He played every day for me, practically. I would sit next to the piano in a little chair, and he would play a song for me called *Heinzelmännchens Wachtparade*, which was composed by Kurt Noack. 'Dwarf' in German is '*Heinzelmänn*,' and '*männchen*' makes a diminutive, like the little dwarves (or goblins or brownies). You don't use two words here in German, you use one word: *Heinzelmännchens*. They were all dwarves with beards, and they were marching in, and this was on the front cover of the songbook—very colorful. I just loved it. It was such a happy time.

When he was finished playing the piece, he would ask what I wanted to hear next, and I would say right away, *Heinzelmännchens Wachtparade*.

My father's piano was an upright, dark brown in color. The music room had the piano in it, and all the other instruments on shelves. There were two alabaster vases on a stand; quite big. You went through a kind of Arabian curtain from the music room into the living room. There were chairs, so that people could listen, watch and play. He had a *Herrenzimmer* (literally, 'room for gentlemen'), a den, where he had his library, and where he would play chess with his colleagues. The furniture was all dark. Some of them smoked, and the table had a brass inlay with four strategic indentations to use to dispose of ashes. This impressed me all the time.

We weren't allowed to go in and look at his books without permission. If we took a book, he showed us it had to be bound in some paper or something so that we didn't damage or dirty the cover. He would show us exactly how to turn a page—at the top edge, not below. If you had your finger below, you tended to bend it. We had to sit to look at it, and wash our hands beforehand, and not do anything else. Once we were no longer interested, we had to give the book back to my father so he could put it back on the shelf in its right sequence.

Typical German discipline. My father always said, "*Neben dem Stock, Brot und Butter.*" (Next to the rod [stick] is bread and butter.) Good sense and good discipline. There was discipline, but there was lots of love.

Every night both our parents would come to our bedrooms. My mother prayed with me, and my father told me a little story. He'd tell me to be good 'til morning, and the sandman would come and I would soon be asleep. (I would always ask why, if the sandman had really come, there was never sand in my eyes in the morning.)

Sundays, after church, we always went somewhere, to a village or a restaurant. The villages had superb restaurants; first class. They had better cooking than a big hotel. They'd usually have a *Metzgerei* (butcher shop) beside it. Afterward, we'd walk and walk. We'd walk through a forest nearby, and if the birds were singing he'd always invent a dialog for each bird. For example, one might say (as my father would interpret), "Be careful, people are coming," warning the other birds. It was always a joy.

He loved to surprise us with stories. For example, once we were out walking in Mainhardt Forest, near the village of Mainhardt, which is about 20 kilometers south of Öhringen. In the middle of that forest there was a clearing, a meadow; three birch trees stood there. Peculiar, really, so I asked him why there were only three. He said they had once been three girls, but the girls had been bad, and a witch had turned them into the birches because of their disobedience. (When we would later come to that area another time, I'd think to myself, "Oh, dear. I hope I haven't been bad." I was always afraid, and I would promise to myself not to do anything naughty.) Nearby there was a tree house, which hunters used during shooting season. Ah, he said, that's where the witch lived, but she might not be home today—maybe she had gone shopping! I said, "*Gott sei Dank*. I won't be afraid any more."

I had a strong imagination, and sometimes it seemed like I was living in a fairy tale.

My father was always dressed in a suit and tie, and had even dressed that way when he was a student. He was maybe five foot six—he was taller than I am now. He was straight. He was slim. His walk was steady. He didn't wear glasses, but instead always wore a *Zwicker* (pince-nez). He often had a bowtie on. I don't remember him ever having a full head of hair—he had hair on the sides and back, but the top was bald. His face was symmetrical, which made him photogenic. He had a kind, nice face. He smiled often.

When we went for a walk, and when I asked some questions, he would say, "Think about it, and you will know, and then finally, yes, yes, this is why. You remember every day you walk on this street; what does this house look like? What's the color?" I'd say, "I don't know." And he'd say, "You have to open your eyes. This house has this and this feature, so be observant."

My father had three sisters; he was the only son. They all lived to over 80, and the last one died when she was 93. She was buried in my parents' grave, because over there in Europe you can own a grave for only 40 years, and then you have to give it up. That last sister bought my parents' grave.

One of my aunts was named Johanna Majer-Eulenbeck. Her husband, Gustav, was an artist. He painted entire fairy tales on a series of glass slides (each about 2 inches by 2 inches in size), using a microscope and a magnifying glass. He would go to schools and show the fairy tales using a projector. They had a one son, and a daughter. The daughter was a magazine journalist in Hamburg. She met and married a man who was a sculptor, but died from the Asian flu within a year. The son, Siegfried, studied in Sweden, married a girl from Paraguay and moved there.

A second sister of my father, Lydia Zechner, was married to a professor of surgery. He worked in Prague for a time, but when the Russians came closer, he transferred to Graz, in Austria. Both were horseback riders. She was my godmother, and always sent me gifts.

The third aunt was named Elisabeth. She never married.

I was seven or eight years old by 1933, and it had been a happy time in Sülzbach. My father was teaching, and carrying on with his other activities, such as painting. He collected flowers, and painted them. He painted portraits of all his students. He gave them a poem to read, and they would stand in front of the pulpit, and he would draw a charcoal portrait. Other times, he'd make oil paintings, such as of village scenes. We, his children, had to sit for our portraits every year, usually in charcoal. We could follow year by year how we looked with those portraits.

1934 Öhringen, Germany

In 1934, my father transferred to another town, called Öhringen, where he was promoted to headmaster. Öhringen is about 25 kilometers north of Sülzbach.

Before, in Sülzbach, he had conducted the men's choir. Now, he didn't do it anymore, as he was already starting to be ill. He was still an ardent pianist. He played the piano all the time; that was his recreation. Beethoven and Chopin were still his favorites, but he played all kinds of others, too.

My younger sister, Liselotte, was born when we lived in Öhringen, in 1935. I was nine when she was born. Walter was 11 and Hans was 13.

Nazism

I wasn't aware politically. When Hitler started, I didn't even know what he was talking about. His beef was *Friedensvertrag von Versailles* (the Treaty of Versailles that ended World War One).

After Hitler rose to power in 1933, there was only one party, one leader, to vote for. People voted for him at that time because he looked promising. He would stop unemployment, and promised to build highways and factories. People voted enthusiastically for him, although my father did not because he was not politically inclined whatsoever. Anyone in a leading position, whether a politician, teacher, priest, lawyer, they had to be a member of the Nazi party. Whether you had a job with them or not didn't matter; they had to have your name on their list so they could say the whole nation was behind Hitler.

It took two years for them to catch up with my father, that there was a teacher who was not a member of the Nazi party. We were sitting at supper one night in 1935, I remember that, and we were up on the third floor of the schoolhouse, where we lived. We heard footsteps coming up, and my father went to the door. There was a brown-shirted soldier, who said that my father was under arrest and would have to go with him. My father asked why he was being arrested, and was told that he would find out when he got to whatever Nazi office was there destination. He left without finishing supper, and we were all upset: crying and crying. He was interrogated half the night, and came back in the middle of the night. Several were invited to come to testify, but no one could say anything bad about my father. They decided that since he had not joined the Nazi party, he must be a communist. However, they couldn't prove anything, so they let him go, with this verdict: you either join the party, or take the consequences. In those days, the term 'concentration camp' wasn't widely known, but it was known that there was a prison near Munich, called Dachau. People who went into this prison did not come out again—a prison without return. This was the only place we knew where political prisoners were held; that was all.

What did my father do? He had no other choice. He would have lost his job. He couldn't have gotten another job. We couldn't have gone to school. Nothing. Nothing.

He signed up with the party, and he was given a number. It was like being a union member, with monthly dues, but there wasn't a job in this union. Now, also, there were restrictions on him. They came to the house, and looked through his library. The books written by Jewish writers were all taken out. Music—Felix Mendelssohn, for example, was a German Jew, and other Jewish composers—all this was taken and burned publicly, along with other printed materials.

The subjects my father mainly taught were math, German, grammar and singing. He was forbidden to teach religion in school. Throughout Germany, a teacher had to greet their students with one arm raised, and saying, "Heil Hitler." My father disliked this, and just flapped his hands instead.

He sometimes went to visit friends in Marseille, and he subscribed to a French newspaper before Hitler stopped it and he couldn't get it anymore. I asked him why, but he said it was just the rules.

My father said that Germany was in economic ruins after the war. He came back to a ruined, pathetic country. Until Hitler came to power, there was massive unemployment and Germany was always struggling. I'm sure he was watched all the time.

Failing Health

My father taught in Öhringen for only two or three years, before he had to retire due to ill health. Because of his illness, he was just too weak. He had pernicious anemia, which is an autoimmune disease: his own body destroyed his red blood cells. He stopped working, and the only thing that he did was play the piano.

Later on, when my father was already sick, Hitler had made Volkswagens available. He offered the Volkswagen as the people's car for a relatively small number of marks, so that not only rich people with their Mercedes and Opels would have a car. The first Volkswagen came out in the mid-thirties, and I saw it an exhibition for the first time. You had to pay a down payment to get your Volkswagen delivered. The actual deliveries became later and later, as time went on. Some people put their money down, but never got a Volkswagen, because the war started. That was one of the ways Hitler got money. He said it was your duty to the fatherland. But the people signing up for a car didn't see that money any more.

My father paid the money for his Volkswagen, but never got the car. Instead, he got a motorcycle. This was when he was already retired at age 46, due to his health. We went outside where we lived in Öhringen, and we went to the country where there was a small creek. The creek had a little falls there, and we would sit in the water, letting it run over our feet. And then he was telling me stories, and about the fish. He enjoyed this, and we just enjoyed each other's company. Then we collected watercress, because it was high in iron, and that's the kind of thing he ate. In those days, there was no supplemental vitamin B12 to treat his pernicious anemia. He lived on raw liver, dark green vegetables, olive oil. Every month he got deliveries of supplies: oranges from Spain, fresh pineapple and bananas. This is what my father lived on, because there was absolutely nothing that could help him. His blood was more and more destroyed. A blood transfusion lasted maybe three days, and then the benefits went right through the kidneys—it didn't last long.

My early life was happy, but I wasn't happy when my mother went to the hospital, or when my father had to go away so many times, for treatment for his blood. My father was treated in a hospital in Stuttgart, starting about in 1935. Every time we said goodbye to him there, it was tearful. My mother would take one child with her to visit him there every Sunday, alternating among the oldest three. We went by train. He would be there for weeks at a time, after which he'd come home, and then have to go again. He was there maybe two or three times a year (as was my mother later, also in Stuttgart).

When you're a child, the severity of your father's or mother's disease didn't sink in. So it was nice being on the train and going for a trip. After visiting at the hospital, we would go to a restaurant to have something to eat. (The first time there, we had some chicken. I was going to take the bone in my hands, and my mother said, "No, no, no. You don't take the bone in your hand." She showed me how to debone it with a fork and knife, and to this day

I don't take a chicken bone in my hand.) It was more an adventure, than just visiting my father. Later, when he was really sick, I never left his side.

Sülzbach was a happy time. But Öhringen was more a sad time, because my mother was sick, too, and quite often in the hospital over Christmas, with congestive heart failure. I don't know what the diagnosis was, but you don't usually have heart problems when you're in your thirties. She likely had bad heart valves, possibly from rheumatic fever as a child, or maybe an enlarged heart. Your heart can hang on for a few years with that kind of disease, but then it wears out.

My mother. *Mama*. I had her for a little more than twelve-and-a-half years. Out of those twelve-and-a-half years, she was in the hospital over four Christmases because of her heart disease. So, I was able to celebrate with both my parents, completely, only nine Christmases in my life. Those Christmases without my parents, even though we had a maid, were sad for me. My father tried his best.

One night I had a dream that my mother had died. My bedroom was next to my parents' bedroom. I cried, and my mother came. She sat on my bed and she said, "Oh no, don't you worry. God will help us. The angels will look over us. Don't you cry. Don't you worry." Ten days later she was dead.

I was already in public school, and my two brothers went to another school, the gymnasium (high school). On Monday, April 25th, 1938, about eight o'clock in the morning, I was already in my classroom at school. My brother Hans came and said, "Come home with me, something bad has happened." I assumed it was my father that was in trouble, because he was always sick. My brother told me, "No, it's our mother." So I went home, and there was my mother, dead.

There were two steps up, and there was my mother's coffin. I could see.

Of course, after that my life was sort of in a fog; it's nebulous for me, the whole thing. I couldn't believe it. It was awful, in those days, seeing the coffin in the house. They closed the coffin and they put those nails in. I can still hear it, to this day, the lid being hammered on with those nails.

After the funeral, when I returned to school, I was in that fog.

My father's illness was why he gave up when my mother died—he just didn't have the strength to go on any more. I was with my father as much as I could. I was his sunshine, in a way. He was depressed sometimes after she died. I just thought he was being serious. He lost interest in eating. Before we went to bed in the evening I was always sitting with him and hugging him.

After our maid got married in the year before my mother died, my father had advertised for another maid. A girl from Vienna answered. In the meantime, my mother died suddenly, so he wired a telegram asking the maid in Vienna to come immediately, since the lady of the house had died. She wired back saying if the lady of the house wasn't there, she wasn't coming. So there we were.

On May 22nd, the next month, I was still in bed. It was a Sunday. My older brother came to the door of my bedroom (again, poor Hans), and he said, "Our father just died." After that, I don't know, the world for me was…gone. We buried him in the same grave as my mother. My oldest brother, Hans, he was so distracted that day. You know when you throw the earth in on the coffin? He accidentally threw his leather gloves in the grave, too.

After our parents died, everything was gone—compassion, guidance, love. I wish I would have known more; I would have been more aware of things. I was completely surprised when they died.

An angel (or my parents) was watching over me through the spirit of God. I knew it must have come from a higher power—why did I have a feeling, right away, if the company I was in was not right for me? Later on, I thought it must have been God's guidance. He compensated for the loss of my parents by giving me good people, and the sense for good judgment, based on my parents' foundation and good influence. I've always thought that God rewarded me for the loss of my parents. Who knows?

Our home in Öhringen was not far from the center of town, where the market square included a church and a monument. Every year there was a carnival, and a midway. That summer after my parents died, I went to the carnival by myself. It became night, and there was nobody to tell me to go home. I didn't even enjoy it, the freedom I had. I suddenly realized that I needed guidance, I needed to be told. It was another real awakening for me. I wasn't even 13 yet.

Before, my parents would have said, "It's enough; it's time to go home now." Before, I didn't want to go home, because I couldn't get enough. But now…

4. Schooling

1938 Öhringen, Germany

The biggest trauma was the first trauma, when my parents died.

Afterward, the four of us children, we were sort of all by ourselves. Then came the fiasco: what happens with us? Fear of being divided was what happened to us.

Of my father's three sisters, only Johanna—she was a schoolteacher, too—had children, a boy and a girl. So they tried to figure out who of us would fit into whose environment. My father's sisters wanted to be nice, but one person couldn't take all of us. We children didn't want to be divided, though; we wanted to be together. We were afraid that we would have to go to an orphanage, and an orphanage in those days did not have a good reputation. They were poor, unpleasant, just like a prison. We worried, we sat together, we cried; we didn't know what to do. We lived in terrible, constant fear. Every day we were afraid that someone was coming to take us. You were afraid for your life.

We didn't know that my mother had inherited money from her mother—my mother was the only child. We had all the fear, about going to the orphanage, about being divided. We didn't know our parents had money. Money had never been mentioned or discussed.

Something else that was traumatic for us was the insurance. There was an insurance agent who came to our house, and looked over the contents, what we had. We were together in a room in our house, and someone came and went through it. We thought it was a very, very bad intrusion. It hurt us that they came and were looking at things, and making a list of what we had. My older brother, who was then just 16 years old, took him by the collar and said, "Please, leave this house. Don't touch anything." Somebody had come, and touched things that belonged to our parents.

This carried on for weeks. The three sisters couldn't decide, and we four didn't want to be divided. My maternal grandmother (I never knew my father's mother), who lived in another town, she finally came after a month and took things into her own hands. She was an aggressive woman, actually. It so happened that, by God's intervention, next to her house was a house available with an upper-floor apartment. She rented it for us, and arranged for a housekeeper. She came one day with a mover, and she said to us, "Here, do you want to come live with me, in the house next door to me?" "Yes," we said. She packed us all up.

So, that problem was solved. No orphanage, and not divided.

1938 Ilshofen, Germany

Well, then, starting in July of 1938, Ilshofen was where we lived. It was also a small town of a few thousand people, about 35 kilometers west of Öhringen, and about 100 kilometers northeast of Stuttgart.

It was not an easy thing, our life then. Our parents were dead. I was in a permanent shock during this time. The reality around me wasn't real, because my parents had died. When I had to go there, to Ilshofen, I asked the movers, the men who moved our furniture, "Oh, please take me back to Öhringen again." But they said they couldn't do that; I'd have to stay. I was so sad.

Now, you'd probably go to a psychiatrist or find similar to help you get over the shock. There was nothing like that for us. We had to go through all that trauma and grief ourselves. My brothers were just as sad as anything.

My two brothers, my sister Liselotte and I had a housekeeper at the house our grandmother rented for us in Ilshofen. Downstairs lived some other people. We had to call the housekeeper *Fraulein*. She saw to our care, going back to her own home after we were in bed.

My brothers were older then, and often studying. I remember lying in bed, and hearing my brothers reciting Latin as I fell asleep.

We looked after each other. Liselotte had bad whooping cough when we were in Ilshofen. She was in the same bedroom as me, and had terrible coughing spells. I was the one who held her up in the middle of the night. I had lifted her so she wouldn't choke when she coughed, though I had no idea what I was supposed to do. I discovered that rubbing her back helped her to cough the phlegm out. I looked after her—I was already a little nurse. I was somehow able to help her, and the doctor came during the day.

Grandmother

My grandmother was so strict, like a general, and not like what you might think of a loving grandmother. I was afraid of her. She didn't hug us like my mother and father had. She told us the way we had to sit, the way we had to stand. When we'd walk in the town, I could not turn around to see who was behind us, because it was not ladylike. I still wasn't allowed to whistle, because my grandmother said it was not ladylike, just like my mother had.

My grandmother was a fighter, and had no patience for weakness. When I cried and begged the movers to let me go back with them to Öhringen, it was clear I did not want to stay with my grandmother. This must have been doubly embarrassing for her. Perhaps that contributed to her never seeming to show any love for me.

But she had a good heart—when anybody needed something, they would go to my grandmother.

She had money—she owned many houses, and a successful restaurant which her brother ran. It was on a river in southern Germany, and herons would come every year to nest there; it was a big attraction.

Her first husband, my grandfather, was a German officer in the First World War. She married twice—her first husband died in 1930, and her second husband died in 1940. She had one child, my mother.

My grandmother—*Grossmutter*, we called her—had a good figure, and a full head of hair. She had all her teeth at the time of her death, at age 79. She paid attention to her figure, and she dyed her hair. In those days, the coloring used for hair dye didn't last long. We were never allowed to look into her bedroom, and one day I decided to see why I couldn't. There was towel on the pillow on her bed, and it was black from the coloring. When the color went out, she would go to the hairdresser again.

This got her into trouble one year, 1914, during the First World War. My *Grossvater* (grandfather) was in the military, and he was stationed not far from where they lived. He phoned her and said his group would be staying where they were for three more days, before being sent to the front. He suggested that she come to visit, as he had a place where she could stay. My grandmother did go, but by then she didn't have time to go to the hairdresser. In her passport photograph, her hair was completely black, but by the time she was set to leave, it was already faded out and the front was all grey. She went anyway. It happened that the German military police were searching for someone on the train on which she was traveling. They arrested my grandmother. She was interrogated for a few hours, and it turned out they were looking for a Russian spy who was dressed as a lady. My grandmother had a big hat on, and was elegantly dressed, and she fit the picture the police had of the spy. They eventually decided she was the wrong person, and that she usually had her hair dyed. After leaving the police station, and arriving at the place her husband had been, she was told his unit had left a few hours previously, and transported somewhere closer to the front. She was so angry.

My first grandfather, I remember only vaguely. The second one worked in the office of a railroad in Schwenningen, where he was an administrator. He had lost most of his hearing on the railroad, but he liked to read, and he liked to do 12-pin bowling. He was a gardener, and a perfectionist. He had particular shoes he liked to wear to church on Sundays, and he was always dressed impeccably. The shoes were cleaned by my mother's maid on Mondays. If she put the shoes in the wrong place afterward, he would correct her. "The Sunday shoes go there, the other shoes go there."

They read a lot, and listened to music and the radio in the evening. He had a record player that had to be wound up to play. Every Sunday morning at six, he got up and listened to the concert that was broadcast from Bremen. Since Bremen was a port city, the program was called the *Hafenkonzert* (harbor concert). He enjoyed those concerts.

Having worked on the railroad, he had lifelong free train tickets, so he could travel anywhere. He and my grandmother liked to go to Lake Garda in Italy. Before they would leave for there, it was like they were going to move house: the luggage! There were so many dresses and clothes, for all possible occasions—it was a 'big do' when they went on holiday.

My mother had always been elegantly dressed, because my grandmother was an elegant lady. She was fashionable. She wanted to put me in a corset so that I'd have a good figure. My grandmother was the best customer of the millineries, and for every outfit she had a matching hat, or had one altered to suit. There was one room with nothing but boxes of hats. The bedroom that had been my mother's before she got married was filled with hat boxes. My grandmother had more guest rooms, so she didn't need to rely on this one, which is why she was able to fill it with hat boxes.

Her house (and our rented one beside it) was on a square up on a hill in Ilshofen. The square included the church and the minister's house, so the hill was called *Kirchenhügel* or *Kirchenberg* (church hill). She had her own personal seat in the church, with a sign that had her name on it.

My grandmother was a colorful lady, and led a busy life. She visited, in Ilshofen and other towns. She went shopping. She went to the hairdresser's. She had people in. Her house had a telephone, which was rare, so people came to use that. People came to her for advice. She helped a lot of people.

My mother and grandmother got along fine. They would never have argued in front of us, regardless. I don't know how much my father liked her. I was sent there sometimes for a school holiday, when I was younger. Once I stayed with her when I was seven or eight, and she wanted me to have a sleep every afternoon, but I was never sleepy. I pretended to be asleep, because I had to. When my father came to take me back home, I yelled with joy when I saw him. I don't think my grandmother liked this, and I think my father might have thought she was too strict with me. They did talk to each other, though. I didn't notice anything amiss, but I don't think they were overly emotional or affectionate with each other.

BDM

I was a member of *Der Bund Deutscher Mädel* (The League of German Girls), or BDM, which was only for girls. The equivalent for the boys was *Hitler Jugend* (Hitler Youth). I became a member before I went to boarding school. You got the notification, and you had to join. You had no choice—you had to, once you turned 14, and your parents had no say. If they refused, they would get in trouble; you could even be expelled from school.

The girls' uniform was a white shirt with a brown skirt. There was a brown sort of scarf around your neck, knotted with a brown leather band. Everyone was young. You never thought anything of anyone. It was a duty, and you did it. It was what we had to do.

The young men and women of the Hitler Youth and BDM held meetings every week or month, where they were indoctrinated about Nazism and Hitler. (My father had avoided having anything to do with these meetings by setting the time of the practice for the men's choir he conducted to be the same as that for the Hitler Youth meetings. He got away with it.) We, the girls and the boys, had marches to do in the middle of the night to learn how to orient ourselves in darkness, and we were not allowed to speak to one another. We had to learn songs. We had to be not afraid of anything. We had sporting events. We had to be strong. Everything was set toward having strong youth.

Everybody showed up at the meetings. They talked about Hitler and how he devoted his life to Germany, and how he would keep us strong. We, the youth, were the future, and everything was meant to make you strong for that future. You had to listen to Hitler speak, although I never heard him speak in person. (He never went far from Berlin or Berchtesgaden in Bavaria, because he was afraid of being assassinated.) Whoever was in charge, when he spoke, when there were open-air speeches on Sunday afternoon, you had to listen. They'd talk about Hitler and the Nazi party. Most of the time, I couldn't even understand a word of what they'd been talking about. In the summertime, you had to start out with the anthem, with your arm out like in the Caesar's salute. After that, you had to stand there in the sun in your uniform, and some people fainted. I was impressed by the Red Cross, and they would carry those people away in a stretcher. I always thought I would like to faint, because it looked like fun to be carried away. I tried, but I never was able to faint.

In Ilshofen, the Hitler Youth assembled in the town square every Sunday at ten o'clock—the same time as church started. The first time this happened, my grandmother was walking to church as she always did, because she lived so close. The church bells rang thirty minutes before church began—nine-thirty. She came but she couldn't get through because the boys were standing side-by-side in a line, close together. She turned around and said to the leader, "Don't you teach your boys any manners?" The leader told them to separate, and she could was able to pass through. From then on, every Sunday she came at the same time, and the boys without ever being asked would open up their line.

Changing Times

I went to school there in Ilshofen, and my two brothers went to regular high schools until they graduated. They took the train every morning back to Öhringen; it was a walk of a kilometer or two to the station from where we lived.

The Second World War broke out in September 1939, when Germany invaded Poland.

During the war, after we children had gone, the American army came in and captured my grandmother's town of Ilshofen four times. Three times, the German army threw them out. Back and forth, back and forth, so that eventually everything was destroyed.

She was down in her cellar all the time then. During the first artillery attack, a shell went through her living room and took a couch with it out the front wall, which collapsed. The couch ended up in the middle of the street, intact. She had hidden in her cellar during the attack. (Household cellars in Germany then were built with a Roman arch, which was strong. If you didn't have a direct hit on the house, you were always safe.) The neighbors told me later that she came out of the cellar after the alarm was over and saw that the top was off her house. She looked at the couch in the street and she was so angry, she said, "That couch stays out there until Hitler comes personally to remove it."

Eventually, her whole house collapsed. The rented one we four children had lived in was destroyed, too; blown up.

My grandmother had a new one built on some property she had opposite to where the old one was. She built the new house without any official permission. The mayor, who was a friend of hers, came during its construction to tell her that she couldn't do that. She told him, "Nobody asked me when my house was destroyed, so I don't have to ask anybody when I build one." This new little house had just a living room, bedroom, kitchen and bathroom, with two storeys. (It was small—after it was finished, her first visitor was the mayor, and as she greeted him she remarked, without humor, "Please come in. I have seven rooms in one kitchen.") It was still standing there five years ago (2007), but the roof had fallen in.

We lost everything.

❊ ❊ ❊

In the spring of 1940, my oldest brother Hans graduated from high school, and he was immediately enrolled in the military (the army) two weeks later—he had no choice, he had to go. So, then there were three of us. Two years later, in 1942, my brother Walter graduated and was enrolled in the army, also—he had no choice, he had to go. (He didn't want to go; he wanted to study at university. A year later, he would be dead at 19 years of age.) Then, our little household in Ilshofen was dissolved.

I was sent to boarding school. My little sister, just seven, was sent to live at the home of one my aunts for a while, to keep them happy. When Liselotte became of high school age, she was sent to boarding school, too.

1942 Stuttgart, Germany

The School

In 1942, I was enrolled in Villa Berg, a boarding school in Stuttgart.

My grandmother found out that the government had opened this private school, and she enrolled me. The Villa Berg was a political establishment. It was just girls, and there was an equivalent for boys, too. They were being groomed to be ambassadors and politicians. Since my parents were dead, my grandmother figured it would be good for me to be in an environment with other people. It was the best she could find; for her, it wasn't about ideology.

My grandmother hated the Nazis, and it was well-known that she was anti-Nazi. (In those days, people didn't use the term 'Nazi;' I didn't hear that until after the war—officially, it was the 'National Socialist Party,' but even that name was never heard.)

It was paid for by the government. There were certain criteria for admission, including oral admission tests. There were girls from all over Germany, and I found nice classmates. It felt like 'home' there, even with all the discipline—it didn't bother me.

The building was actually one of two former royal castles, called Villa Berg One and Villa Berg Two. They were in parks across the street from one another. It was a nice building—elegant. We had a music room. There were two or three girls in each bedroom, which were arranged off a long corridor. We had a dining room, and there were, of course, classrooms. One room had a long glass table with a tablecloth that would be set up in the afternoon for coffee.

It was heavily damaged by the time the war was over. When I revisited some 20 years ago (approximately 1990), only the tower was left. It had been near a military base, an armory, which may have led to its being targeted for bombing.

※ ※ ※

Every day, we were awakened by the teachers at six o'clock with a sort of friendly *"Aufstehen!"* (Get up!) call, and then we had five minutes to get downstairs for gymnastics. We slept in common rooms, usually with four beds. You had your gym clothes on your bed, ready. Quickly run downstairs, and then stand in line. They would first check to see that everyone was there, and then we had gymnastics for a while. When that was finished, we went back upstairs and had a set amount of time to wash and shower, and then dress in the school uniform, a brown jacket and skirt with a white shirt. Next, we had to go outside to raise the flag, and from there we went for breakfast.

Classes started at about nine o'clock. We had to listen to the news, and then we had to write a summary of it so they could make sure we had paid attention. We had a break after an hour of classes, for a few minutes. At twelve we had our lunch, and then we had an hour's rest. We returned to class from two to five. At five, there were sometimes sports, held in a big sporting area there. We played European handball, and gymnastics, and did running, broad jumping and high jumping. In the winter, we used the indoor gymnasium.

The teachers were alright, though they were strict. You knew they were the authority, and you knew you couldn't cross the line. You knew you had to be on your best behavior.

We had some free time before supper, and then we had to go outside again to lower the flag. There was always soup for dinner. Often it was a one-pot supper—everything cooked together, meat and potatoes. There was fruit, apples mostly, or jelly or pudding, because they were easy to do. After supper, we had homework. The lights had to be out by ten o'clock.

They had us always thinking; we had no idle time. Everything was timed: 'Hitler time.' It was almost a military-style boarding school. On the weekends, we couldn't just sit around in the evening and do nothing. We had to use our heads. One thing we did was, each Sunday one class served dinner to the others (during the week, we were served by the staff). We had to learn how to serve, and remove the dishes afterward. We had to decorate, and be creative. We would use whatever was available. We had to put out name cards so everybody would know where they were to sit, and also so the same people don't always sit with each other. You had to figure out something unusual. One class made a picture of a rose, and then said, "Find the matching picture." The other would be at the seat where that person would have to sit. Our class came up with the idea of quotations, so when someone came in the door, they might receive a card that said, "To be." They had to find the matching card, which in this case was, "Not to be," at the table place where they were to sit.

There was no choice regarding what subjects to study. There was math, chemistry, history, geography, German, music, art and languages. I played the piano, and we all sang. There was a school choir, and I was a soprano. I got a good education. Geography, history, art and music were my fortes. I wasn't good at the sciences. We were allowed to go on trips to see Roman architecture.

We took French, but we were not allowed to speak it away from class. There was a French song we liked, but we were not even allowed to sing that. It might give you away as an enemy of the fatherland. Under Hitler's system, everything was different.

In the summer we could be outside. Since the school was in a park, we could walk around during our free time. In winter, there was no skating because it wasn't cold enough, and we didn't have skis.

Every year there were sports festivals, and we had to compete in sports against other schools. Girls competed against girls, and boys against boys. You had to 'exceed' in sport. You had to be strong.

We had a Romanian official come once to visit our school once, because he wanted to use it as a model for Romania (which was 'affiliated' with Germany at the time).

There were parents' nights—not many parents were able to go there, though; usually, just mothers. Nobody came for me. Everybody else had a mother or an aunt or something. I knew that it was hard to travel, because the trains were not available for civilians. They were mostly used for the military, so it wasn't easy for my grandmother to come. I felt that pain, not having anybody coming to see me, and all those various emotions you went through. We performed, made plays, for the people that came, and entertained them. I took part.

One friend, Evelyn, was from Frankfurt am Main. She was a piano player. She planned to carry on with her piano after graduation as a career. There were people from Saxony, and from North Germany—they spoke High German. I still have an album with pictures and names. (After the war, we had all gone home to our different places, but we tried reunions. The ones that ended up behind the Iron Curtain[1] later, there could be no reunion with them.

We had fun in the evenings. Boys weren't the thing, because we didn't see any boys. We'd help each other with homework. We talked about things, perhaps about something a teacher did, or what we were going to do when the war was over. I said once that when the war was over I was going to turn all the lights on, because every night you had to have the blinds down for the blackout—no light could come out of the windows. We also talked about food, and about how when we graduated it would be good not to be told what to do.

One girl was engaged, and we thought it was out of this world, being engaged at 17. When I wanted to go to a dance for the school, my grandmother said it was better to make yourself scarce than to go to everything that's going on.

Thank heaven that I had a foundation of morality given to me, that I didn't fall into bad habits at a vulnerable age. Anybody could have tried to get me into trouble, but I heeded my parents' upbringing. I wouldn't have wanted to bring any shame to my parents. Not anybody was good enough for me. One time, a girl set me up on a blind date. The girl had a boyfriend. Boys didn't come to the school at all, except for the one that was engaged. But my friend, she was meeting the boy secretly. She took me, and said her boyfriend had a friend, but I didn't like that fellow whatsoever, and I left. I said, "I'm going home." He just wasn't good enough for me. I didn't waste my time on anybody or anything that wasn't my 'style.'

It was in the afternoon, and we went to a movie. During the war, if you wanted to go to a movie in the winter, you had to bring a piece of coal with you, so that the movie house could be heated. If you weren't 18, you weren't allowed to go in. The police went into the movie house, and inspected row by row. If they looked at you and saw that you were not old enough (you had to have your passport with you, so they could check), they pulled you out and you had to leave. In those days, if a man kissed a woman in a film, it was a big

---

[1] The figurative western border of the Soviet Union and the countries it controlled.

thing. Some films were not suitable, and you couldn't go if you weren't 18, even though the so-called adult content would have been boring to a ten-year old

One annoying incident to me at least was; we had to go swimming in an indoor pool facility about three blocks from the school. We had to walk on the street in formation and sing. We had to pass by an armory. Whenever the soldiers heard our thin voices, they laughed and made fun of us. With the top of my voice, I harmonized to make it sound a little stronger, but I was not amused.

I visited my grandmother sometimes while I was at boarding school, because my little sister was with her for a while. She helped me by giving me money.

At the boarding school, there was never any discussion of God or religion. We didn't pray or think about God. It was just non-existent. You would have stood out like a thorn. Over time, you forget about it. God was probably with me all that time, but I didn't even know. Where did I get the strength from? Where did I get the judgment from? How did I know not to get into bad company, to know not to do something bad, or steal? I always thought my parents were watching over me, too. My approach to morality came from my parents. Everything I was, and am, came from my parents.

My older brother could paint and do portraits. If I had the opportunity, there are many things I could have learned and done.

All the other girls had their parents. I wondered about what was going to happen to me. You lived your days, though, and I didn't think about it until that official came and they enrolled me in the Red Cross. I wanted to go as far as possible away, to get away. I wanted to see something else. I've always loved to travel.

When we had vacation, the whole school went all together and slept somewhere, such as at a hostel. Teachers, too. In the summers of 1942 and 1943, we went to a hop farm during a holiday from boarding school, to help with harvesting, haying and other jobs, because all the men were away at war. The owner of the farm, a rich man, asked the school for the assistance. We were told that we were all going to a holiday on the *Bodensee* (Lake Constance). There were about sixty of us (the whole school), and we were happy to be going.

The farm was out in the country, not far from Friedrichshafen, and produced hops for the beer industry. It was obviously well-established, since there were living quarters for all the workers. We were assigned one of the residences, which were nice, solid houses.

The hop vines grew high, on heavy strings and poles. There were men with long poles with hooks on the end. They could lift the string, and the hop plant would come down with it. Once harvested, the hops were light, and in no time you could have a big basketful, though it might weigh only two pounds.

We had little stools, sitting in the fields, and we sang many songs, all together. '*Lore, Lore, Lore*' was a good song for girls of seventeen or eighteen, picking hops. There were lots of songs then composed for soldiers. Germans were greatly accomplished at composing beautiful songs and melodies, like 'Lili Marlene.' (That song was enjoyed by many other countries. 'Lili' and 'Marlene' were two girlfriends of a soldier in the First World War.) There were songs for infantry, songs for sailors, songs for the air force, songs for sailors in submarines. When soldiers sometimes marched through the streets, singing, all the local girls would open their windows and doors, waving.

So, there were songs, and laughter. At lunchtime, we'd all sit outside at tables. In the evening, we would sit together and enjoy the outdoors. We couldn't make a campfire (no light allowed—blackout rules), so we were sitting in the dark, and singing. I had grown up in German wine country, around Sülzbach, and it wasn't usual for children there to get half-wine, half-water to drink in their home. (And, of course, the white wine was good for my father's illness to drink every day.) When company came, you'd always offer a glass of wine. In hospitals, they'd give out wine, too. I don't think we got wine at the hop farm, because Hitler was sort of against alcohol.

(Drinking alcohol was different in Europe then—different rules. You didn't abuse it. You learned wine was a social thing. You didn't get drunk on wine, which goes with the socializing. You didn't get out of hand. If someone got tipsy, say in a wine pub, they simply wouldn't be served any more, because the owner would lose his reputation. If anyone was drunk, they were looked upon as 'low' people. That was another deterrent. There were wine festivals, where people were selling their own brand of wine. You bought a glass with the first drink, with an emblem of the winery on it. Where my oldest brother lived later, in Crailsheim, they filled the city fountain with wine for their annual wine festival. The wine in the fountain's recycled in it, of course.)

The hop farm owner had a small light hidden for us, that couldn't be seen from an airplane. We were right on the shore of Lake Constance, on the German side, and over there we could see Switzerland, ablaze with all the lights. The lake is not that big, maybe two kilometers across. We were envious, and said to each other, "When the war's over, we'll turn all our lights on!" We were dreaming about what it would be like.

We were there until the holiday was over, and then we looked forward to the next time. It was a really nice vacation; relaxing, a nice change, and we were happy.

I always clung to people when they were nice to me. Another time our school went on a hiking trip through Bavaria, and we slept in hospices. At one hospice in Bavaria, there was a husband and wife who looked after us. There were just bunk beds with straw to sleep on. The food was simple—there was cheese, bread, porridge and milk for meals. It was high up in the mountains where they lived, and that's all they had. They herded the cows from the villages all around in the summertime. (That's why Swiss chocolate and Swiss milk are so good.) In the fall, they went back to the farm again. The wife was so good and so kind to me. After a few days, when we left, I was the only one who cried, because I was so touched that someone had been so nice to me. The other girls weren't in the same situation I was, and I felt good that I had a 'mother,' at least for a short time.

Hitler

In the 1930s, Hitler came to power, and suddenly, jarringly, there was a dictatorship. People had to be careful in what they said. People were afraid to talk.

Hitler made a big impression at first, because he was everything for the workers—introducing the Volkswagen; anybody with four children getting the *Ehrenkreuz der Deutschen Mutter* (Honor Cross); free railway trips. It was thought that he had the people behind him. I thought as a child that Hitler was a good man, although I never really knew what he was talking about. You had to listen to his speeches, in the home, in the school, in the factory. Later on, people began questioning his decisions, such as marching into different countries. My father was still alive when Hitler took over Austria in 1938, and I heard him saying, "He can't do that, that man brings us to war, because you can't just march into somebody's house, and not have him do anything about it."

We were so hyped up in the school with propaganda that you thought that what he was doing was right. But, I began to wonder, toward the end of the war, when they announced on the radio that Germany had a new weapon and could drive the enemy back again, I began to question it. When the war was finished, I thought to myself, "My goodness. How in the world can we have all been so blind? How could we have followed him and believed in him?" But it was too late.

Germany had a capable propaganda minister, the Jesuit-trained Dr. Goebbels. His speeches were exceptional. He was a well-educated man, with a good command of the German language—he spoke beautiful German, and his voice was more pleasant to listen to than Hitler's. He was a 'good' propaganda minister, because he spoke only of hopeful things.

It's too bad that the Americans condemned them all, or even charged them; they should have left them to the Germans. We would have been happy to deal with them. You begin to wonder how we could all have been so pliant, but then we found out about the concentration camps. When I found this out, I couldn't believe it. I couldn't believe it. I asked, "What is this? What is a concentration camp?" I had no idea.

One of Hitler's main interests was to have the youth in good shape. They had to be physically fit, so sports were promoted. Hygiene was promoted. Young people got special food rations. Everything was about 'the youth,' because that was his future, the platform to build his Reich on. It wasn't frightening. The youth were looked after.

As long as we followed the many orders we were given, we had no problems. If they told us in the school, "That ball is black," you said, "Yes, sir." You didn't say, "No, it's actually white." There was only one straight line to follow, and you knew you could not divert from it. "This is where you have to go; this is what you have to follow." It was actually easier to just obey.

We were so indoctrinated about Hitler, about what a wonderful man he was, how he devoted his life to the people. You believed it. "He lives for only the people, that's why he doesn't get married; he doesn't have time for that." He was a hygiene nut. He was a vegetarian, so he promoted this for healthy living. Every week, in the school, we had our toothbrush, comb and shoes inspected, to see if they were all clean. This was all under his orders. We knew the rules, and what to follow.

The school staff told us what to believe, and we wouldn't have dared not to believe it. You didn't talk about it, because you didn't know who you could talk to. As an example, a child may have been asked, "Why didn't you come for the youth meeting?" "Well, my mother said I had to go to church." "Ah, so your mother says church is more important than the youth meeting." Even children could unintentionally give their parents away.

You were afraid to talk to anybody. People could give you away, report you, because then they would be in favor. You had to be careful with whom you speak, and what you say. It was even constantly on the radio, with a warning every hour: "Be careful what you say. The enemy is listening." The actual enemy of the government was their own people.

Everything was such a police state, everything was controlled. They had their hands in everything. Everything.

After war was declared in 1939, the same hour ration cards appeared, so they had prepared beforehand. Everything was ready to go. My grandmother sent me to the corner store for a pound of butter soon after, and they said they couldn't give it to me. I asked why not, and they said you needed cards, ration cards, for butter. I went home to my grandmother, and she said, "What nonsense!" (She was a forceful woman, and she got the butter.)

At first, I thought it was a joke, but as time went on we learned that it was the way it was going to be.

If you were a farmer and you had 100 chickens, it might be stipulated that you had to produce 1,000 eggs over some arbitrary time period. They'd say you'd have to deliver, say,

600 eggs to the store, and you got to keep the other 400 for yourself. Then you didn't get ration cards for eggs, because you'd have them yourself. If it ended up that you didn't have the quota they set, and you were short somehow, then it was just too bad for you. The same with pigs; you were not allowed to butcher a pig without permission, and then they'd say how much meat you'd have to give to the butcher, and how much you could keep for yourself. Everything was regulated—you wouldn't believe it.

It was Germanic, being organized, but Hitler went overboard. He knew what he was planning to do.

I remember seeing an anti-Jewish propaganda film that was released during the war. It was called 'Jud Süß' or 'Jude Süss' (literally, Sweet Jew). It's a strange title; it doesn't make any sense. The Jewish people were represented as taking over everything, and being conniving and corrupting. Films like this showed them with ugly faces and beards, and in the most unpleasant ways. You could watch only the films they wanted you to watch—you couldn't see anything else. We had to see propaganda films. The point was just to underline that we should all hate the Jews.

I didn't hate the Jews. My parents had an older Jewish couple who were good friends of theirs—the Edelbergs. Their son came visiting them around the start of the time that Hitler began being publicly against Jews. The son came to us and said goodbye, telling us that he was going to America. He didn't tell us the reason. His parents were our friends, and sometimes on Saturdays I went there sometimes, and they'd serve me special bread. One day I came home, and heard they were gone. My mother was crying, and said Mr. and Mrs. Edelberg had been arrested and taken away. I asked what they had done, but she didn't know. That was the last we heard of them, but we did learn that the son had made it to the States. We were told that they probably put them on a ship, and sank the ship or something like that. Hitler put out all kinds of propaganda giving his reasons why he should get rid of the Jewish people. They were constantly talking about Jews not being 'clean' (this wasn't in the hygienic sense), and that they were corrupt and dominating. Jews were said not to be a good race, and that Hitler wanted to create an 'Aryan' race. It was all told as simple 'fact.'

This hadn't started in 1933 when Hitler came to power. At first, unemployment went to nothing because he built the highways, the autobahns. Those autobahns weren't paved, they were made from concrete blocks. No one knew that he wanted fast transport for the war. We built those highways, north and south and east and west. And then the factories. People were glad, and workers were happy—they had work to do. They never thought of striking, and they were happy to work without a holiday. He was, at first, for the working class, a godsend. Then, of course…

It started as soon as 1935. When people wanted to get married, they had to bring a certificate saying there was no Jew in their family for ten generations back. Otherwise you couldn't get a marriage license. You couldn't marry a foreigner. If there was one Jewish relative in your family, you could be dismissed from your job. A colleague of my father's, a schoolteacher, had a Jewish wife, and he lost his job. I don't know what happened to them. The man couldn't teach anymore, because he was all of a sudden 'not clean.' If I had asked why, my father couldn't have told me, because it might get accidentally misrepresented by me.

There were a lot of German people who went to concentration camps for speaking out; some of the camps were originally built for German dissidents.

I was brainwashed during the war, as a youth in school. Afterward, you slowly came to the realization that Hitler deceived us, and that he was so strong that he could make a whole nation follow his ideas. It ended when he killed himself, which was even more cowardly. You were built up about being a 'master' race, and it ended up that you had acted as the worst race.

I mentioned the news broadcasts that we had to listen to daily in school. They started out with "*Nachricht*" (This is the news). The news was heard in every factory, school and household, although you heard only the news they wanted you to hear. You heard what was happening in the war, and propaganda about Hitler. Most of it was talk about ideology, and nationality, and the duty that you had. You heard about the National Socialist party, and what their ideals were. They said that Germans were a superior race.

The broadcasts always praised what Germany had done: they marched into this country, and how fast it had happened, and how superior the German military was. They had sunk so many ships, and shot down so many planes, and advanced so many thousands of kilometers. They moved into another country, and there was no resistance, and so forth. At the end they might say Germany had lost three airplanes or something like that, but by then you were so hyped up that those things didn't bother you.

It was always a man that read the news on the radio. At other times of the day, there'd be military music, and the sounds of Germany marching on.

All the students paid close attention so that you could remember what was said. If you didn't, you would get criticized. The test for listening was to make a written short summary, every day. You made notes during the news. The teacher would evaluate the text. They might say afterward, "No, it wasn't quite that way," but mostly they accepted it.

Everyone was afraid. You had to know about Hitler's life, so we learned about it. We would be told things like: how he was born in Braunau in Austria; how his mother was treated by a Jewish doctor; how Hitler painted in Vienna but was turned down by an art school with a Jewish president, and how Hitler always hated Jews from then on; how in order to make some money, he painted postcards, and went around to coffee houses and sold them; how he became interested in politics, and eventually went to meetings, and attended parliament; how he found that Jews were always taking things over. All these things, we had to know. They told us we had be constantly alert, so even if someone woke us up in the middle of the night, you would have to be ready to answer questions correctly. So, you went to bed, thinking about all these things, worried that they would wake you up to ask you. There was constant tyranny.

When Hitler spoke, a radio was brought into every classroom. It was every individual's duty to listen to it. (Except for my grandmother—she said, "I'm not listening to this Austrian gypsy," and she turned the radio off.) If someone had been reported as not having listened, they would have been punished. People wanted to listen, though, because they wanted to know what was going on.

Hitler's speeches to the nation might happen once or twice a year. He was systematic in the way he spoke. After arriving at the pulpit, he stood there for a time, waiting for a while, 'magnetizing' the people. He would get worked up as he spoke, and then stopping sometimes. Hitler didn't have an unpleasant voice, but it was erratic in the way he raised and lowered it. When you could see him (though I never saw him in person), he always gesticulated a lot.

Most of the time I wouldn't even have understood what he was talking about. He talked about the duty of the Germans, and about people having to be strong. The Nazi Party would be said to be working to make Germany an ideal place.

He spoke when Rudolf Hess escaped to England[2], and he pictured him as a traitor, and that he had fallen into a trap. I remember that speech well. I couldn't figure out what in the world Hess was trying to do, negotiating with the English.

Before he came to power, Hitler waited until Germany was up to its neck in water. There had been government after government, and Hindenburg was the leader. Hitler waited until Germany had almost drowned—the unemployment was so bad, the economy was so bad, and that's when he stepped in. Overnight, he practically eliminated unemployment by building highways, by building factories. The first few years looked really hopeful, really good.

The more children you had, the more welfare you got and the more money you got for each child. (My grandmother had a cleaning lady who ended up resigning from her job for that reason.) For people who had a lot of children, there were free cruises on ships in the North Sea. There were railway tickets, and discounts, to keep the workers happy. It was Hitler who built housing subdivisions for people, to get them out from the inner city, because tuberculosis was prevalent.

When I was still in boarding school, everyone had to give up their fur coats. There were piles, mountains, of fur coats in the armories. Furriers cut the coats into mitts, hats and coats for the soldiers at the Russian front. Girls and women had to help to sew these things; I remember we would put a little letter in the pocket to greet them when they got a coat. (Soldiers coming home from the Russian front later told us they never saw any fur; perhaps it had been sabotaged.) People didn't dare not to give. It was their duty, to the Fuhrer and to the fatherland.

Then came a call for skis, because they said the skis were needed for troops fighting in Norway. If you had skis, you had to give them to the army. After that, you wouldn't dare to use skis if you still had any.

Any strike was impossible. People worked without holidays, for years, and they wouldn't dare to strike. They were right behind Hitler, at first, because Hitler gave them work, jobs, money. For the working class, he was good. Eventually, they woke up themselves when they saw how the war was going. By then, it was too late.

He ruled by fear, by oppression, instilling terror by doing things like arresting people. Even spitting on the street was verboten. The police checked hotel guest lists, and if a couple shared a room and were not married, they were arrested. Known homosexuals were shot; this happened to one of Hitler's friends under his order.

Living in War

The food was rationed, but we got enough food. There were no imports—we had only what was grown in Germany. Meat was rationed, of course. At the school it was different, but for families it was a big deal to have (or not have) a roast for a Sunday.

I found out a lot things after the war that I had no idea of during it. For example, my brothers, I didn't know their address or where they were so I could send mail to them—on the envelope you just wrote their name and their military service serial number. I didn't know my older brother was in Russia. I had a classmate, whose husband was killed by a prisoner in a concentration camp. She didn't find out until after that war that he had been an SS[3] guard in the camp.

---

[2] Hess was Hitler's deputy as Nazi party leader; Hess parachuted into Britain in 1941, in a failed attempt to independently pursue peace.

[3] The SS—an abbreviation for Schutzstaffel (protective squadron)—was a large organization in Nazi Germany with broad police and military presence and power.

You got used to it, and put up with it, because you couldn't change it. I sometimes slept down in the air raid shelter. I was constantly in fear.

The mayor of the town where my grandmother lived was her friend. He had to be a Nazi; otherwise he wouldn't have been a mayor. He was Catholic, and went to the next town to go to church so they wouldn't know. My grandmother didn't give him away, because they supported each other. My grandmother knew some people who were Communists before the war, and became Nazis during it.

I was as surprised as anyone when the war broke out. I was 14 years old, and was probably in school when it was announced. I knew from my father, who knew from being a prisoner of war in World War One, and being mistreated, that in a war, people are irresponsible. When it comes to actual war, people can have power over you, and they can hate you, and you're the enemy. I knew it was harsh, the way they had treated him, and that it had been severe, and that it would be again.

Nonetheless, we didn't know what was going to happen. Immediately, the propaganda was such that when they marched into Poland, they said it was successful. When Hitler kept on going, I knew it was bad. We didn't know where it was leading to. As a child you don't have that much comprehension, but I don't think anyone knew what to expect.

All these changes were happening, without people being asked. There were just orders and rules. This is what you did, and this is the way it was going to be. We knew there was nothing we could do. You couldn't discuss it with anybody, except maybe my grandmother, but I wasn't with her much. Adults didn't discuss things like this with children. I didn't have any family structure—I was always with strangers. I made friends, but I didn't really get to know them. The whole thing wasn't normal, to begin with, but the circumstances were such that I didn't have family to lean on.

We were told that the English had bombed us, so we were going to be bombing them. We heard about Pearl Harbor, and we thought maybe the Japanese would help us. I don't know whether or not I wanted Germany to win the war. I just wanted to stay alive, and get out of it. After two or three years, you really got sick of the war. Every night, you had to make your windows dark. There were many restrictions and propaganda all the time—always asking us to be strong. Hitler never said what would happen after the war.

One time late in the war I had a conversation with an air force officer in an air raid shelter. I asked, "This invasion of Europe, where is it going to lead to? They are already in France. That's not far from Germany. It doesn't take long to get here from there. We're going to be shot." He said, "Don't worry. We have some secret weapons. It just has to be used." He wouldn't say what it was, but I think he believed it himself.

The defeat of the German army in Africa was a great disappointment. Erwin Rommel[4] was a hero to everybody, until he lost in Africa. He was respected; even the British general Montgomery had respect for him. He was a fair commander; he wouldn't allow any prisoner of war to be mistreated. After his *Afrika Korps* was defeated, he took over at the Western front. He had lost his reputation, and the SS didn't even take his orders—the SS was Hitler's army. When Rommel saw the idiocy of the SS strategy, which had gotten more SS soldiers killed, he spoke to the SS officer in charge, the commandant. But the commandant said, "I don't have to take your orders." That was the difference between

---

[4] Rommel was a general in the German army, popular at home for his early World War Two victories in northeast Africa against the Allies. Defeated at El Alamein in Egypt in 1942, he later commanded the German defense of the English Channel coastline. After the invasion of Normandy in June, 1944, he was implicated in the July, 1944 plot to assassinate Hitler, and forced to commit suicide.

Hitler's SS and the regular army. Regardless, Hitler didn't even listen to his officers—he always thought he knew better.

My Brothers

I have a loss of memory for the whole month after my parents died. I don't think I was talking much with my grandmother during that time, because I was so disturbed. In comparison to my parents who hugged and kissed us all the time, my grandmother didn't as much. I couldn't confide in her because she wasn't inclined that way, somehow; I didn't have emotional support from her. Some people you feel comfortable with, some you don't. Generally, if I asked, she would give advice. Our relationship was not strained, but it was such that it wasn't easy for me to confide in her. In a way she loved me, but it was more duty.

She loved my brother Walter. (He could get away with anything!) I remember doing something wrong once, although what it was I have totally forgotten. My grandmother was going to reprimand me in a furious tone, but Walter, who was her favorite one, intervened for me.

I confided in my grandmother's maid for a while, but then I was told that I couldn't do that. Nobody really supported me until I was in boarding school, when I was with my classmates, my peers. But, even then, there weren't any adults. I shied away from people who didn't appeal to me; I was a recluse.

I had to work everything out by myself. It's a good thing I have a sense of humor. This was sort of a power which was overpowered by my emotions, but eventually my sense of humor took over, so I could absorb everything. I had to absorb everything by myself; I had to work out everything by myself. My brothers were depressed, and they were in another school, and eventually they went off to war.

The younger of my brothers, Walter, before he was sent to Africa with the *Afrika Korps*, he was put into a company where everyone was 'officer material.' He was ready to go to Africa with Rommel, when his whole company was called to go to Yugoslavia[5] and clean out a partisan area. He was the first one in the company that got killed.

Once when he was still in Germany, he sent me a picture of a girl, and asked me, "What do you think of that girl?" He wanted my opinion. He didn't have a girlfriend then, but this girl was sending him letters.

He had come home for a visit in 1942, and I went to the railway station and waited to welcome him. When you're young, your brothers think you're silly once they become adolescents. You don't play together the same way anymore; you don't look at each other the same way. But when he came out of the train station and saw me, we both threw our arms out and ran toward each other. We were happy; that was the first time we met in a mature way, and we got close. It was the last time I saw him.

After he was killed, all my grandmother got was a letter, which she told me about later by phone (I was in Stuttgart at that time). She had a service at the Lutheran church said for him; she knew his favorite hymn was *Ave Maria*. She seemed slightly upset when she phoned, but I was more upset. When I hung up the phone, I just cried and cried. I just thought that it was the war, and what could you do? I was surprised. It was horrible that it happened to him. I was close to him; we were only two years different in age.

The letter said, "Walter Speidel died for the *Führer* and the Fatherland. *Heil Hitler*." He died near Zagreb in Yugoslavia. He was killed in a forest by a sniper, and buried near Zagreb in a regular cemetery. After the war, my oldest brother went to Zagreb to look for

---

[5] A country comprised of a varying amalgam of Balkan states, in existence from 1918 to 2003.

the grave. He was told that when the Russians came through and found that there were German soldiers buried, they dug up the graves and took the boots off the dead bodies. He never found Walter's grave; it had probably been destroyed. Walter was the first one in his company to die. He had written to me in his last letter, "We are waiting for orders, and I wanted to take the opportunity to write to you," before they were ordered to go into that forest and clean it out of those partisans.

I didn't really think much about dying. I just had to accept that Walter was dead, just like I had to accept that my parents were gone. It was just one more thing. I was missing him, of course, but I never nurtured a grudge or anything further, because I knew I didn't want to get depressed.

We played always well together, my brothers and me. Walter liked to tease me, but if another boy was teasing me, or something like that, he would defend me, even to the point of starting a fistfight. If anybody did anything to me, he would really let them have it.

We would sit together on his bed, and tell stories, like the Karl May Indian stories. I read the books, too; they were really fantastic. Once we were talking about children a lady we knew had; at the time, my mother was pregnant with my little sister, ten years after I was born. I was so naïve. There were many storks where we lived; they lived on nests on top of the chimneys. We were told that the storks bring the babies, and if you put out sugar on the windowsill and it's gone next morning, that means that you've been chosen to have a baby. My brother said that men give birth to boys, and women give birth to girls.

Walter didn't want to go to war, but he had no choice. He was stationed for a while in Stuttgart, in an armory not far from where I went to boarding school. On Sundays, everyone in his unit went out in the town, but he would be sitting in the armory, studying books, because he knew he would miss out on further school. He wanted to be an engineer, and to go to university. He knew the war would make him miss time for his education, so he wanted to study to get a head start.

No one wanted to talk about being afraid to go to war. Everyone hoped they'd get home again after the war. No one wanted to talk about anything that had been put in place by Hitler. You were afraid to express your opinion. It was a police state, so you were careful what you talked about. Some thoughts simply didn't occur to you, because it was not your concern. My oldest brother had been in the war already, and he had survived, so my younger brother probably expected the same outcome for him—he might just come through.

Hans, my oldest brother, didn't talk about his feelings about going to war. I couldn't talk with him about it, and neither could his son—there are many things his son doesn't know, but would like to. Hans still had two bullets in his lung after the war, because it was thought better to leave them in than take them out. He was also shot through his right wrist. The fingers on his right hand were not straight; they were stiff and were pointed in all kinds of directions at once. He couldn't put his fingers together. Through physiotherapy he was able to regain some use, and eventually was able to play the violin again. He was right-handed, and after the war, as an architect, he needed to use his right hand. You could always tell by the way he held a pencil, that he had a problem from the nerve damage. Later on, he had a lot of arthritis and pain in his wrist and hand. Finally, he had been shot through his right thigh. The bullet carried some of the material of his uniform with it, and the exit wound was large. He needed skin grafts, which he got in France in a military hospital as a prisoner of war.

He was wounded in a battle in France, sometime after D-Day. I don't know where. I didn't even know he was in France—he had been in Russia before. He was still in a hospital in France when the war ended. I found out only after they released him, after the war, when I returned from Austria to Germany. I didn't know where anybody was.

My brother Hans was always more of a thinker, and the night my father died he stood by the door, holding it, and the imprints of his fingernails were left in the wood. After that, he was changed, his personality changed. He became more serious. He never talked much. In his old age, I knew he had cancer of the prostate, and when I phoned to talk about it I said, "Hans, tell me. What is the matter with you? I know you're not well." He said, "Don't you worry about me. Once I can eat properly, I can get my strength back again. You have enough problems." He died soon thereafter. He wouldn't tell me on the telephone. This is how he was. He kept everything inside. Walter and I, we showed everything on the outside; we showed our emotions.

Graduation

Shortly before we graduated, some kind of government official, I don't know who he was, came to the school and talked to us about what we could do after graduation. He was in a military uniform, and a typical official—'feeling big.' When he came in, as for any visiting official, we had to stand up and say, "Heil, Hitler." You'd be tense, because you didn't know what to expect. He was businesslike, and acting like an authority.

He told us that as girls, we had three choices: we could become a railroad or streetcar conductor, work at an ammunition factory, or join the Red Cross.

Railroads and streetcars were likely to get knocked out by bombers and snipers. You couldn't even go on a train near the end of the war, because they were always being used by the military. There might be one car for civilians, at the end. A lot of them were destroyed. On a bus or streetcar, you couldn't travel in a straight line to anywhere, because there were always many detours resulting from the constant airplane and artillery bombardments. Houses and other buildings in Europe then tended to be made of stone, and after the bombing there would be big heaps of debris everywhere.

I didn't want to be blown up at an ammunition factory, or shot at or blown up on a train, so I decided to join the Red Cross. They had their own hospitals, and their own schools, and the Red Cross nurses were looked after by the military. They needed help, so I would be able to get a fast education.

Boys had no choice. They were enrolled in the military on graduation. My older brother Walter was in the infantry. My oldest brother Hans was in the *Panzer* (tank) division in Russia. (Hans told me after the war that in Berlin once his tank drove by where Hitler was standing and watching the parade go by. All Hans would have needed to have done was make one hard right-hand turn to drive into Hitler, and that would have been the end of it right there.) He was pulled from Russia and sent to the Western front before the invasion.

Every university faculty was closed except medicine. If you were past third year, you could continue with medicine, but you were also in the military, and after lectures you would go back to the military base.

I knew I at least had a goal to do something. I was told there was a chance. It was a relief. I could never rely on anybody for help.

5. Education

1944 Vienna, Austria

After my last high school term was finished, I first returned to visit my grandmother in Ilshofen. It wasn't long, maybe a week or so, before I had to leave. They called you right away.

I had chosen Vienna to train for the Red Cross, though there were other places I could have gone in Germany and Austria—I said right away that I wanted to go there. Even then, I was dreaming of getting away and traveling. We couldn't go just anywhere—Germany was still at war, but Austria was still united with Germany. I would be trained as a nursing assistant, because by then they didn't have time to train you for a full three years to be a nurse.

By train, it's normally about seven hours from Stuttgart to Vienna. However, sections of that rail line had been destroyed by bombs, so I had to go via Prague. At the time, Czechoslovakia[1] was still occupied by Germans. I arrived in Prague in the middle of the night at the north train station there, and I had to get to the west station to catch the train to Vienna. Unfortunately, I did not know my way around the city at all. There were people sleeping on the floor in the stations, soldiers and refugees, and you had to practically climb over them. I asked several people if they could tell me where the next station was. They said either "I don't understand," or "No." I was sure a lot of them spoke German, so I wondered why they wouldn't give me information. But then I realized they hated us, we Germans, because we were occupying their country. It was another shock to me. I had never been hated. I had to find the information by myself. I couldn't speak Czech. I couldn't ask anybody, where this-and-this particular railroad station are, because nobody would answer me because I was German. I walked through Prague in the middle of the night. I knew to go west, because I had to get to the west station. By the grace of God, and my guardian angel, I found it.

I felt hurt that nobody would tell me directions. I wasn't actually afraid; I was so naïve I guess, yet I wasn't used to people hating you. I was just 19 years old.

Arriving in Vienna for the first time, it was all new to me. I thought I would have to just find my way around—that was the only choice. It was like a new adventure.

The address I had to go to, for the training school, was in the fourteenth district of Vienna, near Schönbrunn. I was on a streetcar, and I heard someone call out "*Brigittenauer Brücke*" (the name of a bridge over the Danube),' and I thought someone was calling me personally, so I got up. I felt like a fool! It was just a regular stop for the streetcar, at that particular bridge.

There was no traffic, no automobiles. Can you imagine cars, then, for heaven's sake? The only cars that were allowed to run on gasoline in Germany itself were for high officials. For other people, you had to build a little wood stove on the outside of the car, and use it for fuel. To go up a hill, you had to get out and push because the engine wasn't strong enough.

The Red Cross was sort of an independent organization, from the government. They had various agencies. They looked after military hospital services. They administered the distribution of 'care' packages.

They gave us shoes and a uniform. We lived at the same place as we studied, following a specific curriculum. We were glad that we could continue with our education, with a roof over our heads. I was able to quickly assimilate in with the rest of the students.

---

[1] Former union of the Czech Republic and Slovakia.

I don't think we got paid while we were trained, but we did get food and shelter, and our uniforms. You were used to strange food, and getting only a little of it. It wasn't really a concern after a while. I didn't really have any possessions. I had a suitcase with some clothes, and a few mementoes of my parents and my brothers.

For the residence, they had put up ready-made barracks, with bunk beds. The accommodation was generally good there. Vienna often got bombed—the American air force had only to come from nearby Italy. Usually I had a lower bunk bed, but one time I had the upper bunk. In anticipation of air raid alarms, beside your bed you had all your clothes ready, because it was dark and you'd have to get dressed in the dark. I forgot I was on the top bunk, and I casually stepped out of it, and fell all the way to the floor below. By time I collected myself, everyone had gone.

We had classes in first aid, and basic anatomy and physiology. We learned how to bandage, and how to look after a broken arm. We saw wounded soldiers, and you had to look after them whether you were prepared or not. You sort of learned on the job. You knew the basics.

There were people who became romantically involved, because they knew they might never come back. It didn't matter whether they knew the person for long or not. There were not many men around—they were gone. That's why so many women had to do jobs that men would have done otherwise. There were some men, such as those with heart conditions who couldn't do active military duty. When the soldiers came back home on furlough, they would go out in the evening, dancing and going to restaurants. There weren't organized dances; they'd go a nice wine pub, and they wanted to dance, so they got up and danced.

We were all in the same boat. You tried to laugh, to have fun. After each bomb attack, you had your own thoughts, such as "Well, I survived that." You had to keep on living. Some funny things would happen, and you'd laugh about it. You didn't walk around sad, or crying. It was normal to us; it was the way you lived, given the circumstances. You adjusted. We still had some fun, and laughed when we could.

There was nothing of God yet for me. I didn't start to embrace God until I was at the Catholic hospital in Wels.

Vienna was beautiful. We tried going to the opera; fortunately, it was still going on, because the soldiers needed some entertainment, too. We were able to get only standing room at the Viennese Opera House. One night there was a performance of 'Madame Butterfly,' and the Japanese ambassador was there with his wife, who was wearing a kimono. Wow. We didn't know until we came out of the building that a red carpet had been laid out. It was the icing on the cake. There were movie houses, but you still had to bring coal in the winter. Most of the time, there would be an air raid alarm during the film, so you rarely got to see one all the way to the end. Germany had a good movie industry, before the war and the ugliness Hitler brought.

Vienna and Stuttgart were different cities. Vienna was 'the' city of culture, though it changed after the war. Stuttgart had ballet and an opera house (which was completely destroyed in the war). I got to know the atmosphere in Vienna, the Viennese character, through one of my girlfriends, who was a native. The language was different—it was German, but kind of a melodious dialect. I didn't notice much difference in the language. Viennese people could tell I was German, but they did not treat me differently. I had no problems that way.

You never knew what was coming next with the war. There was a lot of destruction, so you knew there would have to be a lot of cleaning up. There were many people buried in the rubble of the houses.

I had a good friend while I was in Vienna, Annalisa, who had previously been a medical student. Unfortunately, she had not yet entered the third year of the program, and so she had to leave and work with the Red Cross. We remained life-long friends. Five years ago, the last time I was in Vienna (approximately 2007), she had developed Alzheimer's disease. She was married to a physician who was a heavy smoker; he died of cancer of the pancreas.

Near the end of my training, I was told that I would be going to Wels, Austria, to the hospital there. There was no choice; you did what they told you, and nobody questioned it. I thought it would be a new thing, and I would just have to put up with it. It was a relief, really. It was something to go to. I knew I wasn't expected to be in charge or anything.

I was there until the war's end, although a lot of things happened in the meantime.

1944 Wels, Austria

I went by train from Vienna west to Wels on August 30, 1944, which was a journey of perhaps an hour-and-half. I hadn't been to Wels before. I knew there was a castle there, and that it had a reputation as a lovely city.

There was no one to meet me when the train arrived at the station there.

The Hospital

When I arrived at the hospital, they knew all about me, about what I could do. They assigned me to a particular floor, telling me a particular nurse was in charge, and if I needed any help to go to her.

The Wels hospital was called the *Kreis Krankenhaus* (district hospital). It was a solid building; it's still there (although it's now called the *Klinikum Wels-Grieskirchen*). It was a Catholic hospital, then, and was managed by an order of nuns; they're still there. I knew about hospitals from having visited so many times when my parents were sick. My mother had been in a Catholic hospital, too.

The hospital was a big building, with high ceilings, thick walls and wide stairs. There was a lovely chapel. About two-thirds of the hospital was for military patients, and about one-third for the public, although all the patients were treated the same. There was a unique atmosphere created by the nuns; it was a special ambience they made—peaceful, orderly, organized.

The nuns were told they could have nurses from the Red Cross, as well as nursing assistants like me. Red Cross nurses could be in charge of their own military hospitals, but they were never in charge at the Catholic hospitals.

We worked 12 hour shifts, so we were tired when we were finished. We had a half-day off a week, and we would sleep, or do some washing. We ate at the hospital; the food wasn't bad. The nuns baked their own bread, and it was good. Pea soup, of course, and pasta (they made it themselves). The German and Austrian custom did not include dessert, though there might have been fruit. At four o'clock, you might stop at a coffee house, and have some coffee and cake. We got some cookies sometimes, and every morning we got a little whisky from the Mother Superior—she didn't want the Americans to get it when they arrived. We thought it might provide a little defense against the typhus. I was protected—I could easily have gotten typhus or tuberculosis. Hitler had been afraid of tuberculosis, which is why he had subdivisions built. He wanted to get people out of the city with their small spaces, and get them to subdivisions.

I was so impressed by the nuns, their habit, and the long outfit. I was impressed by the way they carried themselves; they gave you a comfort. I even went to the Mother Superior and told her I wanted to become a nun. But she just laughed and said, "No my dear, you're just influenced by the environment and overcome by events." But there was such a peace in that hospital!

There were old and young nuns. One of the older ones had a little office. I went in one time without knocking, and she quickly took whatever she had been eating out of her mouth and put it in a drawer. Did she eat something she shouldn't have? I pretended I hadn't seen, and just left. The older nuns did some funny things.

One of the young nuns was named Sister Angelica, and we became friends. We had fun. One soldier was kind of romantic, and kind of wandered around and talked to the female staff. The mattresses there came in three pieces, rather than a single pad like now. Sister Angelica and I took the middle piece out, and put a basin of water in its place, and then covered it with the linen, pulling the sheet over so you couldn't see. He went and sat right in the water. We were into mischief sometimes.

Sister Angelica was Austrian, slim, and wore a full habit like the other nuns. It was a long white garment, with an apron. She was pleasant-looking, perhaps 27 years old. I wore my Red Cross uniform, which was gray with a white apron. I didn't like what I looked like then, because I had gained some weight. (Sometimes it seemed like we got nothing to eat but pea soup, pea soup and pea soup. I usually didn't mind it, but I soon had enough for a while.) I still liked myself, though.

I found peace at the hospital—the whole atmosphere; all the nuns prayed. They did not get upset, they were not afraid that they might get hit by bombs. There was a big red cross on the roof, so they didn't actually get bombed, even though there was a military airport nearby. (Some hospitals were bombed, and some not. Churchill gave the order not to destroy Heidelberg, because he studied there himself once. One of the hospitals I later trained at in Germany was partly destroyed. Much of Wels was eventually destroyed because of the airport and the railroad freight depot, which was a large station for freight and passenger trains). I said to Sister Angelica, I'm always afraid of getting killed. She said, "Because we pray, we're not afraid of the bombs falling. We know that God will take care of us. God helps us believe that we will be safe." This made me think, there is something I was not familiar with. I wondered how this could be, that they felt this. When you came from the outside, it was so peaceful—no noise.

The nuns did wonderful baking. On certain days, there would be special cookies or pastries, and everyone looked forward to those. The staff from all the other floors came, too.

I learned a lot about medicine. I learned not to panic, to address problems the right way. There was no formal training—you learned on the job. There were always new things you had to cope with, but you could ask the nuns-nurses for help.

There were many amputations, I remember. There weren't enough doctors available to save the legs. Sometimes I was called into an operating room to help hold a limb so it could be sawed off. The first time I had an amputated leg in my hand, I almost fainted—it was such a strange feeling.

There were many abdominal wounds, too, but most of the patients were orthopedic. Many patients died from blood loss. The suffering bothered me. I wondered about the families of the men who were badly wounded, whether they had a wife and children. We tried to get the patients' thoughts off their problems, and talked and joked with them. A lot of the patients walked around with crutches. Some were optimistic. Many were happy to be alive, because they knew they didn't have to go back to the fighting.

When I talked to Sister Angelica and asked her whether she was afraid of getting killed, of getting hit by a bomb, she said first of all there was the red cross on the roof. She said they knew God would take care of them; they had complete confidence. I wondered what kind of a force this was, that gave these women such faith. It made me think. When I observed them, and saw them at their mass, I thought if that was what they did, I wanted to do the same thing. Later on, when I went to the Protestant church, it seemed empty; it didn't give me anything. I tried it again for a while when I got to Canada, but it was still empty.

God was somehow in my mind, but I didn't consciously think about God every day. It made a big impression on me, that there was something that could give you that strength of mind. There must have been a higher power. I realized that it was God. I got more and more involved with it, and more and more embraced it. When I eventually returned to Germany, I went by myself to Catholic services, even midnight mass sometimes, rather than go to a Protestant church. I felt there was someone there I needed to impress, and I prayed, mostly the Our Father. Later I learned the Hail Mary, in German, but now I say it in English. Eventually it evolved, and it got more and more developed. It didn't come all of a sudden. Someone told me there had to be a higher power—look around at all that's been created. Flowers, and nature; it's not just by coincidence.

There were people who went to church, but they would be pestered by the authorities. My grandmother told me she knew a Catholic who went to church, and who was constantly hounded by party members, trying to find something to use against them.

There were still Italian troops fighting alongside the German military, directed there by Mussolini's system. The Italian monarchists were by then with the Allies, but the fascists still fought alongside the German army. Like the German soldiers, the Italians came to the hospital if they were wounded in fighting nearby. They might spend a night or two to be stabilized; once they were ready to be transferred, they were sent to their own Italian facilities. (In those days in Germany, they called it a *lazarett*, meaning a temporary hospital.) The understanding was that it was only for war situations, since there wasn't a nearby Italian hospital. If an Italian soldier was at the hospital for even just one night, and transferred out the next morning, they would still leave a love letter for you under the pillow. They made promises, and marriage proposals, and told of having been away from women for so long.

There was one wounded Italian soldier, perhaps in his thirties. He was alone in a recovery room, because he had tuberculosis. He was my patient, and he became quite amorous. He said that he wanted to marry me, but I knew this was just the circumstances. It wasn't realistic. One day he pulled me toward him, wanting to kiss me. I went to the nun who was in charge, and told her I wouldn't go in there anymore.

There were also Italian soldiers stationed at the hospital, manning the anti-aircraft guns on the hospital roof. When there was an air raid alarm, some of them wouldn't go to their stations on the roof, but would come down to the basement shelter with everyone else (they were often the first to arrive). They would have been punished by the Germans, if they had known. There was one fellow who had a terrible nosebleed, which I treated for hours before it stopped.

There are different kinds of nosebleeds. If it's dry in the winter, the mucous membrane can break and start to bleed if it's not properly lubricated. Another type is bleeding in the sinuses, and there can be so much blood lost with that type that a blood transfusion would be needed. As a nurse, you can end up spending many nights on call with a patient with a nosebleed. They may swallow the blood; they may vomit the blood; they may need a transfusion; it's difficult sometimes.

I had no idea how to treat this particular Italian solder's nosebleed, so I just used common sense. I put ice on it, and spent a long time trying to help him. After two hours, it finally stopped, and from that moment on he called me *amore* (darling). He was one of the soldiers who were supposed to be manning the anti-aircraft guns on the hospital roof. Whenever he saw me in the hall or on the grounds, he'd call out, "*Oh, Amore, Amore!*" If I saw him coming, I'd go quickly in the other direction.

I don't remember whether he was good-looking or not. You weren't 'tuned in' to that kind of thing. Now, in peacetime, if a young girl sees someone, she might be interested. But then, your mind wasn't on this. You had a different attitude toward everything. There was not much flirting, though the younger nurses may have. I really had no time for teenage dating, so I was still naïve. I had not had many dates.

Some soldiers used any opportunity they could for 'romance,' like when they were on furlough, or if they had to stay overnight at the big railway station in Wels before the next train came. Any woman they could find, they'd try to have an affair with. They probably thought, who knows, tomorrow they might get killed, so they decided they might as well use any chance that arose.

When I started at Wels, the soldiers who came to the hospital had been transported there from field hospitals. On arriving, some of them had already had treatment done, such as having a limb amputated. Those who needed immediate attention would be kept there, with the less urgent cases being sent away to be looked after later. There came a time when it was no longer possible for casualties to first go to a field hospital. As the American and Russian armies got closer, wounded soldiers were sent directly to the nearest 'real' hospital without treatment. They were not dressed first, or cleaned up, or looked after at all with primary care. They arrived at our hospital directly from the battlefield.

We had to go out and receive them, and load them onto stretchers to be taken into the hospital. One day there was an officer whose whole face had been shot off—destroyed. There were no more cloth bandages available by this time; instead we used ones made of paper. His face had been dressed with these paper bandages, and there was pus running out. I couldn't see any of his face, other than his nostrils. When he heard my voice, he asked me to reach into his coat pocket and get his pistol out for him. I asked him why. He said, "Do I have to tell you?" I didn't give it to him. I started crying, and went to talk to a colleague nearby. I told her I couldn't do it, because the man wanted to kill himself.

All the incoming soldiers were badly injured. There were no proper bandages and few supplies. The physicians were distraught, with one even crying, because they had no medication to give for pain relief. It was grim during those last minutes of the war. Antibiotics like penicillin and streptomycin were becoming common elsewhere in the world, but there were none whatsoever that day in Wels.

One night I was sitting with a doctor while he wrote his reports. He got a phone call from another doctor in the hospital, and was told the good news that there was some of the antibiotic penicillin available. He was surprised, because he had never heard of it. After that he was called 'Dr. Penicillin.'

The soldiers didn't talk to us (the hospital staff) about the war, though they may have talked among themselves. They were so glad to see women, have clean clothes, and eat warm food. They were happy and joking, and glad to be alive. Some worried about not knowing where their families were, as there had been no correspondence for over a year.

You couldn't send a postcard or a letter. They might wonder whether their wives were still alive, or about whether their wives knew if they were alive. They all had their worries, such as not knowing how they would get home, and not knowing what they would find when they got there. They spent a lot of time thinking about their future.

The soldiers in the hospital were usually in their twenties, though there were some who were older. The soldiers were relieved to be there, to have 'made it.' They were delighted not to be fighting any more. Some said they hadn't even wanted to go in the first place. There was general happiness and relief, which made for a good atmosphere in the hospital.

Officers and soldiers were treated differently. Officers usually had their own rooms, whereas soldiers wouldn't. Despite this, everyone received the same level of health care. Before the war, there had been a class distinction—depending on what you could afford, you could be a first-class patient, second-class patient, or public. In the public section, there might be ten beds to a room, with two or three per room for second-class and single rooms for first-class. Patients could order and pay for their food *à la carte*. The old hospitals had large rooms for the public patients, whose beds would be separated by curtains.

Austria was full of lakes, and there were many hotels on those lakes. Once the wounded from our hospital had sufficiently recovered, they would be sent to one of the hotels for rehabilitative therapy. The hotel owners would have to give them up for military use.

I often swam in Lake Fuschl on my day off. It was near a village called St. Gilgen, in the *Salzkammergut* (salt cave region), which has many salt mines nearby—hence the name of the nearby city of Salzburg (salt castle). (The lake is shown in the film 'The Sound of Music.') There was one hotel after another along the shore line there.

There was a Polish doctor who had first come as a patient, but wanted to stay on at the hospital. He ended up befriending a nun; after the war she eventually resigned, and they got married and emigrated to the United States. It was a surprise, and caused quite an uproar. The nuns were highly secretive in those days, but you could tell that they were upset.

I was seconded for a month or so to work at the Wels railroad station, because of the bombings there. My job there was to distribute vouchers for food and drink to the soldiers passing through—the soldiers who came for their ration cards had to go to their own special lineup.

One day an English airplane was shot down nearby, and one of the pilots parachuted safely and was captured. There was a German army officer in charge of the railroad office, so they brought the pilot there. The German officer was from Munich, and he spoke English, so he interviewed this pilot before he was taken away to prison. (It so happened that the German officer was a Jehovah's Witness—I never knew how he was able to keep it a secret from those who would persecute him for it.) My own first reaction was to wonder whether the pilot was hungry; I wondered if I should ask him if he wanted something to eat. But I wouldn't have dared. It was my enemy. I wasn't used to hiding anybody. I didn't really harbor hatred. This was war. We were at war. They were at war.

You were afraid to talk to officers of the government, though they weren't even interested in you unless you were a threat. One nurse friend of mine had a brother who was the Protestant archbishop of Oldenburg, or some similar diocese. He preached against Hitler and ended up in Auschwitz, and it was officially announced that he had supposedly died of a heart attack. His sister would say only, "I don't know if I can believe that."

The City

When I first came to Wels, we were housed in a temporary wooden barracks. It was about five kilometers from the hospital, and we walked there and back—that's why we made shortcuts along the railway. We made curtains from gauze we got from the hospital, which made it a little livable. After a while, it was blown up in a raid, but not when we were there—if there was an alarm we wouldn't have stayed there anyway. We were at the hospital, and we heard the area was bombed, destroyed, and there was nothing left. What little I had was destroyed, too.

We were moved to another makeshift barracks. There was no heating, so it was cold. Sometimes, we slept with our clothes on, because of the air raids. We slept on straw, or their might have been thin, primitive mattresses. You didn't care who had slept there before, although we never saw bedbugs. The blankets were the typical cotton military ones. One blanket wasn't enough—they weren't warm.

We ended up living in three different barracks, before we were moved to a hotel. It was right in town, opposite the railroad station, perhaps two kilometers from the hospital. It was an ordinary hotel, perhaps three storeys high. There were no windows, and the roof was gone. This was the only place where we could sleep. The military simply told the owners that they were taking it over. They used the kitchen to prepare food for soldiers, and we used the guest rooms for sleeping. Some of the floors were destroyed, and there were no paying guests. (I visited there long after the war ended, and the hotel is running again, and is still right opposite the railroad station.)

Although there was food available at the hotel for the soldiers, all we could get there was soup. The soldiers were friendly. They would make small talk with us—"Nice to see you. Where are you from?" But nothing was normal.

We had soap for us to use, but it was hard soap, like laundry soap. There were toothbrushes, but you had to hang on to them because there were no replacements to be had. Many times you didn't have toothpaste, so you'd just use soap.

We were on the top floor—since there was no roof, there was no ceiling. When it rained, we had only one umbrella each, so we didn't know whether we wanted a dry head or dry feet. I usually decided in favor of the head.

Sometimes, when a train arrived at the station opposite, there would be a bombardment, an air raid, and people would be killed. To get the bodies away from the station, they'd put them in a courtyard that was behind the hotel. The first time I arrived at the hotel, and looked out the window to the courtyard, I saw all these dead bodies, just lying on the ground. It was the way it was. You were stunned, but what could you do? I didn't like it, but I was able to sleep despite it—I had to.

I lived at the hotel until maybe two weeks after the war ended, when the Americans came, and then we stayed in the hospital. Some floors at the hospital were divided up, and everyone found a bed somewhere.

We were afraid the Russian army would arrive in Wels first. We wanted the Americans to come first. Linz, on the Danube, where Hitler grew up, was where the Russians eventually stopped. It was spitting distance from Wels. If you lived in Linz, and worked in Wels, you couldn't go home any more. We heard shooting day and night, and artillery. Russia didn't have a big air force, but they still were able to send three or four planes; the sound of their bombs was different, and they split up into a thousand little bits. They did more damage this way. When the Russian planes came, you just took cover, because you knew what would happen.

I did well at the hospital. It was the best time for me during the war. I felt protected, and had a roof over my head (during the day, anyway). There was camaraderie with everybody, because everybody was in the same boat. The willingness to help one another during wartime was so good. As soon as the war was finished, everybody was by themselves again, looking out for themselves. During the war, everyone was helping each other, and comforting each other.

There was no 'having fun.' There were no dances. Even the movie houses were closed. Everything was about just trying to survive. Nights were spent being on alert for bombing raids. You laid in bed with your clothes on, waiting for the alarm. If it went off, you didn't have time to find your clothes. Most of the time there was no electricity.

When there was an alarm at school in Vienna, we went to the air raid shelter. At work in the hospital, later, there were duties to do; you had to help the patients get to the air raid shelter. The alarm was made by a siren, a loud siren, and they were usually mounted on a roof. There was always fear when the sirens started. People would say things like, "I hope they don't come to bomb us;" "When will the war be finished?" "We're all going to die." Once the raid was over, the sirens made a different sound to indicate that.

The city was eventually destroyed. There was hardly anything standing. Just heaps of brick and stone. If a bomb hit, everything around it would have been destroyed. In the center core if the city, buildings were completely destroyed, although there might be the odd wall or chimney still standing. When they bombed, sometimes there seemed to be a specific important target, such as a factory or something industrial. Other times, they bombed the city generally, and it just seemed unplanned.

You knew air raids were coming because you heard the droning of the airplane engines. When the weather was clear, especially during the winter, you could see them coming. You'd hear the sound of the bombs as they fell. The soldiers told us to run toward the bombs if they were coming close, to have a better chance of getting away from the effects. Quite often, we'd end up lying in a ditch, facedown.

Once I was walking along the railway tracks to get to the hospital, and I lay down between the tracks like that, facedown. I hoped they wouldn't see me, because I could hear them shooting over me. It was frightening. I expected every minute to be shot in the back. I didn't pray, because I wasn't then in that stage yet, to ask God for help. That evolved later on.

Another time I was walking on the street, and three airplanes came. Sometimes they'd come after a bombing raid was over, to shoot at people as they came out of hiding. At first I couldn't tell whether the planes were American or German. Some of the houses had concrete walls around their yards, with wire fence on top of that. I heard shooting over me, so I ran over to the wall to lie down, and the shots went over me. They were shooting at people. They wanted to demobilize Germany; they wanted them to give up the war.

The explosions from the bombs were awful. Sometimes the windows shattered.

There were no German airplanes in the sky where we were, especially toward the end of the war. Men were in the infantry, not the air force. There was hardly any defense in our area. There had been air battles before, but there was no such thing after I was out of high school. There were anti-aircraft guns on big buildings, and on factories, and there was one on the hospital (though the Italian soldiers manning it never seemed to use it). You didn't go outside much—it was not a normal life.

The Germans had some Russian Cossacks in the army. We didn't want to meet them. They were really mean-looking. They didn't smile. They just looked at you. Like many soldiers in the area, they came on the railway. There was an office at the railroad station, where the soldiers would have to go to get information about their next connections. If they missed the train, they had to have an officer verify that they weren't deserting when they came back to their company. At the hospital, we sometimes handed out ration cards, so the soldiers could go to a kitchen and get some bread and some soup. The Cossacks came too. They never smiled, they just took the card.

There was an airport near Wels. Despite the red cross painted on the roof of the hospital to warn aircraft not to bomb it, when the nearby airfield was bombed, there was some damage to the hospital. I didn't see any repairs done when I was there, because there was nobody available to do repairs.

Bombing interrupted your daily life. You never knew when they'd bomb. The airplanes came from England or from Italy; once they crossed the border, there was a general alarm. You never knew which city they would bomb. They might fly toward one city, but turn and bomb another. Sometimes you could tell that they were going to bomb your area, because two or three days before, scout airplanes came to take photographs. Sometimes it was during the day, and sometimes at night. The ones at night used what we called 'Christmas trees,' which were burning flares that illuminated the whole city. We'd know our city would be the next one to be bombed. Oh yes, you knew that.

Once there was an alarm, you could go to the air raid shelter. Sometimes if we happened to be outside the city, we could see the bombs falling inside it. I was mortally afraid of being afraid, and of having a bomb fall on me. You'd wonder when it would end. If you survived a night of bombing, you couldn't feel sorry for yourself, but you'd start worrying about whether they'd come again tomorrow. You might be the next one to die, tomorrow.

A lot of the regular army officers were against Hitler—they knew he was a madman. That's why there were so many assassination attempts on Hitler; it could be done only by the command, by the highest officers.

We knew the war would be over eventually, but we didn't know if any of us would live long enough to see it. There were times you never got out of your clothes, because you had to go to the bomb shelter. You didn't know if you'd be able to get dressed, with no light and having to fumble in the dark.

If you had a day off, in any new building you also made sure to know where the exits were, and where the nearest air raid shelter was. You were constantly on the look-out. Life was about avoiding danger.

We had to get up every night to go down to the air raid shelter. The war intensified over time—you'd hear of more damage, more cities destroyed, more people losing their husbands, more people getting killed. You were afraid for your life. You became almost desensitized, hearing about direct bombing hits on houses, and people dying. You'd think it was horrible, but at the same time wonder if tomorrow would be your turn. It wasn't that you didn't care anymore, but you got to be expecting that something is going to happen to you.

With the attempted attack on Hitler's life in July, 1944[2], Rommel was implicated; all of a sudden he was said to be a traitor. Nobody believed it. His car had been attacked by Allied aircraft in Normandy[3], and he was wounded and was at home for a while. After his implication in the failed bombing of Hitler, they came and told him to take his own life[4]. We were told that he succumbed to his wounds from the airplane attack. There was a state

---

[2] July 20, 1944.
[3] July 17, 1944.
[4] October 14, 1944.

funeral for him, so everyone was so sorry, really sad that Rommel had died. His mother and his son had to swear not to say anything, or they would be put in prison. His son, Manfred, became the mayor of Stuttgart for many years.

When Italy was invaded, I thought to myself that eventually we'd be surrounded everywhere, including the Russians, and that we'd be strangled. By then, you didn't know what to think. In a way, you thought it would be over fast, but you wondered what the consequences would be. What would happen to us? We were tired of it. We were sick of it. We were numb from it. We felt humiliated, because we had been on a high horse to start. We wondered when it would be over.

You began to wonder about the Allies coming to the mainland. After the first one, when they threw them back, you thought it would never happen again. I talked to a German army officer I met at an air raid shelter about the invasion of France. I said, "It doesn't look good. If they are already on the mainland in France, what's stopping them?" He said, "Don't worry. We have a secret happen, and we can get them out." I didn't know until after the war what the secret weapon was—the V1 and V2 rockets.

When France was invaded, I knew we were getting weaker and weaker. A lot of factories and industry was getting destroyed. We knew that. There was a shortage of gasoline, and we knew about that. We knew it was just another sign that we'd be overwhelmed, defeated.

In a way we wanted Germany to win the war, but you were caught in the middle, and didn't know what would happen. Each person had their own opinion, but you couldn't talk with anyone. That officer in the air raid shelter was the only one I thought I could talk to, but generally you didn't talk. People didn't know themselves what was going on, but they suspected. The propaganda was still there, but you could put two and two together. They were in France. They were advancing. What was there to stop them?

Christmas

In Wels, there was an immense freight train depot. All the freight trains in Austria seemed to run through there, to be loaded and checked over. There were constantly trains running through with ammunition and other military supplies; maybe even carrying people doomed to the concentration camps.

On Christmas Day in 1944, that whole area was bombed by the Americans. Perhaps there was sabotage, too.

There was an alarm before the bombing started. Some of us were in one of the machinery buildings at the hospital, and a soldier came running in and said, "There's a bomb unexploded out there. Don't go out at the front of the building." So, we went out at the back. Nearby, an officer stepped on a mine, and he was blown up.

That was the night we went out after a train got bombed.

There was a long troop train sitting on the tracks at the depot; it had anti-aircraft guns on the front and the back of it. We found out afterward that there was an order for all the soldiers being transported to stay there and wait, on the train. When it was bombed, fires erupted, and everything and everybody on that train was burned. It was surrounded by trains loaded with ammunition. We were sure someone had told the Americans that the troop train would be there that day, maybe even a German.

Any personnel who could be spared from the hospital had to go there and see if anyone was alive. We went in a military truck, maybe ten of us, including some physicians. We got there about 11 o'clock at night, not long after the bomb exploded. The truck driver dropped us off, and went off to other duties. Our job was to see about the wounded when we arrived—nobody knew if there was anybody alive. It was just outside the city. We heard the explosion from the hospital; it was a horrible noise. The soldiers on the train might have tried to shoot with the anti-aircraft guns.

Everything at the train depot was destroyed. The huge buildings where the trains were overhauled were destroyed. Broken railway lines had landed a kilometer away. It wasn't frightening so much as it was overwhelming—the burned bodies, the smell of burned flesh. It stays in your nose for a while. It's a different smell.

There was nothing we could do. All of the people on the train were dead, burned to death. There might have been a few still living for a time, but they couldn't have lived for long. They were all dead. It was terrible turmoil, beyond your comprehension.

We stayed overnight, because we had no way to go home; we were so tired that we decided we might as well stay where we were. We slept in one of the craters, because it was warm there. It was surrounded by burning buildings, and it was hot, even though it was December. It seemed like a normal thing to do. We didn't go down deep into the crater, staying at the edge. We used the stones to make a bit of a pillow. It was the middle of the night, and the truck was gone, and we didn't want to walk because we didn't know whether there were any mines buried there.

I felt numb.

I think that is the night that I had a nervous breakdown, because when I woke up I was in a doctor's office, lying on an examination table. They said I had to stay there a while. I remember that I was hysterical, that I lost my nerves. I couldn't take it any longer. The nurse who was there said over and over, "*Ziehen zusammen.*" (Pull yourself together.) I think I slept a few nights there, because I was exhausted physically and mentally. It was difficult to sleep on that small table without falling off. The doctor who owned the clinic was away at the war; his wife was in the Red Cross and looked after me. Afterward, I felt OK again and went back to the hospital, and functioned again. I came around, somehow. Nobody ever mentioned anything about it to me.

We worked 12 hour shifts at the hospital in Wels, 7 to 7. After the war, we were 24 hours on, and 24 hours off. We were young, so it wasn't bad.

Years later there was a gas explosion on Monaghan Road in Peterborough, Canada when I was a nurse there. A woman and her three children were at home; the husband was at work. They fell down to the basement after the explosion, and the three children were burned to death. The mother was burned too, all over her legs. They brought her to the hospital, and I was there. Many people stopped what they were doing, to help. Both her legs were amputated. Afterward she had many skin grafts. The nurses there, when they saw this, they were so shocked when they saw those burned legs. For me, I wasn't shocked, because of what I had seen at the train at Wels. The smell was still the same smell. For me, it wasn't the first time I had seen something like this, so I was a step beyond my colleagues.

I was hoping that with all I saw that I wouldn't become insensitive. I think I have managed to do that.

Americans and Russians

We knew the Americans were getting closer and closer, from the west and the south, from France and Italy. We knew the war was going to end, but we didn't know how it would end. We hoped the Russian soldiers didn't get there first—we knew they were cruel, especially to women.

The German army blocked roads with sandbags, trying to keep tanks from getting through. A lot of intersections in the towns were blockaded. Because of this, to go home you couldn't go in a straight line; you'd have to take many detours. At the same time, the Americans bombed, the Russians bombed, the artillery was shooting, so it was changing fast. I had no sense, really. There was always shooting, and you'd always hear artillery.

The German detachment in Wels was ordered to blow up railroad bridges. Three days before the war ended, one bridge had dynamite set on it, but the German officer in command refused to blow it up. He was hung, publicly because of his defiance to Hitler. We were appalled. We felt so sorry for that officer. To order something like this, we were really appalled.

All of a sudden, in early May, 1945, the Americans were in the town, although they arrived before the war ended.

I was often surprised by news of the war. When Hitler got married on April 30, 1945, we heard all the church bells ring. We thought the war was finished, but they told us Hitler got married. We wondered about that, because we had been told that he was not interested in women, that he's devoting himself completely to the German people. We wonder who he had married, and we found out her name was Eva Braun. We were surprised, saying "What!?" After the war, we found out about his beautiful house at Berchtesgaden (which they shouldn't have bothered destroying, because people go there anyway), and how he and Braun traveled there in separate cars. Only his closest friends knew about their relationship. Just days later, we couldn't believe that the war was lost, that Hitler had deceived us about everything.

When the Americans came, we were still living in the derelict hotel near the railway station. I couldn't go the hospital that day, because there was so much shooting. Most of the nurses were Austrian, and some of them just left, to go home. There were three of us from Germany, and we couldn't go home. We were huddled together in the big kitchen of the hotel. German soldiers had shoes with hobnails on the soles, so you could hear them when they were walking. The Americans had rubber soles, so you couldn't hear them. Americans wore brown uniforms, and Germans green. Suddenly, an American soldier in full uniform burst through the kitchen door, holding a rifle with a bayonet fixed to it. We didn't know what he was going to do, whether he'd killed us. But he laughed when we turned around, and he left. We thought, "Oh, gosh!"

A few days later, they came again and looked through the hotel. We heard that they were looking for quarters for them to sleep. We couldn't go over to the hospital to work yet, because everything was bombed or dynamited or mined. We were locked up in the hotel, with just the nuns looking after the patients then. The Americans had also set a curfew.

We were worried that if they came to live in the hotel, we would have to leave. We were sneaky. We put something in every empty room: either a Red Cross uniform or some article obviously from the Red Cross, maybe a bandage or a hat. They came and looked through, but they didn't stay, and didn't come back anymore. They must have seen that it was all occupied. After a few days, we got worried; we wondered what would happen if they found that we were cheating. But by then, we were allowed to go out again, and go to work.

We went to the hospital, and found that the Americans had established their headquarters for the city there. They were good to us, and we started to get chocolate, chewing gum and cigarettes. I smoked then, quite a bit (I quit in 1954).

If we wanted to go out (downtown was completely destroyed, and there was much ammunition lying around and rubble from many demolished buildings), we had to get permission from the Americans first. At night it was too dangerous, but one day the nuns weren't able to bake their own bread anymore—I'm not sure what had happened. A bakery had been established downtown, and someone had to go there from the hospital with a horse and buggy to collect bread. I volunteered. There were *Panzerfaust* lying around (literally 'tank fist;' handheld anti-tank weapons, which were bigger than hand grenades), and rifles, and dead horses, and all kinds of things. It was difficult to get there, but I wanted to see what it looked like. I was always curious.

On the way back, an American soldier came by in a jeep, and called out to me in German (I found out later he was of German descent). I had thought he was going to kidnap me, so I started to run away. "*Stoppen! Brauche keine Angst haben,*" he started. (Stop! You don't need to be afraid.) He didn't want to do anything to me, he just wanted some directions. Because the city was so destroyed, I didn't know myself, so I couldn't tell him.

There were many strange incidents like that.

The war was over, but we did the same things as before, except we needed the Americans' permission now. You knew the war was over, and you felt relieved. There wasn't any big change from what we did before, although food was short. The food got worse after the war ended, and was worse again when I got back to Germany. During the war, pea soup was the main dish, and there was bread. After the war, the Americans from their headquarters would share their breakfast packages with us, just because they were nice or feeling sorry for us. They had their rations dried in packages. Their breakfast included a little piece of chocolate, dry bread and cheese, and other things like toilet paper. They knew that we liked the gifts. (The Americans immediately had local girlfriends.)

We couldn't speak much with them, because of the language difference, but we'd smile at each other in greeting, and say, "Hello." We learned a few words, like 'how do you do,' and 'please' and 'thank you.' They knew we couldn't speak English.

There was a black market in Germany, but not at the hospital in Wels. Anything we needed, we got from the Red Cross, such as our uniforms, clothes, underwear, stockings, coat, hat, blouses, skirts, dress, apron, shoes. You went to a PX, or something like that, for supplies. There were stores in Wels, but the food was only what was produced in your own country, and you needed ration cards to get anything. We didn't need ration cards in the hospital.

I was surprised when the American soldiers who were Catholic came to the mass at the hospital in Wels. This was another eye-opener. The German soldiers would never have been allowed to go to church. After fighting in the war, how could they come? There must have been something higher than human strength that helped them to keep their faith through all that, in spite of everything.

We were all relieved that the war was over. We accepted that, despite the destruction, there was nothing we could do and that's the just way it was. We were happy with the Americans. They were our liberators, in a way. We were no longer afraid of being killed, and they brought new things, new foods—bananas, for instance. The atmosphere had changed. You could sleep at night. You could leave the windows open, and you didn't have to darken them at night anymore. During the war, they had to be completely sealed; there couldn't even be a slit of light that could get out. You couldn't bother to take the shades out during the day, so you were always in a dark room. It was too much trouble. Now you didn't have to do all those things. It was a big freedom for you to open the window, and to be able to turn on the lights, if there was any electricity.

There was a de-Nazification program. The American commission wanted to know who had positions with the party. For example, they asked my grandmother back in Ilshofen, "Can you tell us what so-and-so did? Can you come and testify?" She said, "If I knew, I wouldn't tell you. I am not denouncing my own people. They will be punished when the time is right for it. They will get what is deserved. This is not my role." She was known in her town for having defied Hitler, and for being a personality. She really was. She was an elegant woman. I wasn't approached, as I was too unimportant to be asked anything.

The Russian soldiers were a different story. People who escaped said the Russians raped all the women, and stole whatever they wanted. The Russian soldiers had been given leave to do whatever they wanted with the German people.

There were some physicians who were initially patients at the hospital, and then stayed on and helped after they were better after the war. There was one German fellow who was good at repairing electrical things. He stayed for several months, and was so handy with everything. The hospital was near a railroad bridge, and to get downtown you could take a shortcut along the railroad tracks. He took this route one day, dressed in his German military officer's uniform, since he had no civilian clothes. There was a train stopped there, filled with Russian soldiers being returned to their country from German prisoner of war camps. (There was a rumor that some Russian soldiers protested, since they did not want to go back to their motherland.) The physician was walking along the tracks, when someone on the train shot and killed him.

There was little control over whether anyone had any weapons or not—you could readily find firearms in the rubble. It took a few months after the war before the occupying Allies gained control—until then there was chaos. Many horses belonging to the German military had been abandoned, and were running loose in a field on the outskirts of the city. An enterprising local man gathered them up, housed them at a nearby destroyed military air field, and rented them out for horseback riding. I went riding there myself several times.

Gunskirchen

Patients from the nearby Gunskirchen concentration camp began to arrive at the hospital almost as soon as the Americans arrived. I felt so terribly guilty, that the Germans did this. I almost took responsibility for it, and I apologized to two Hungarian patients who had been physicians—I said, "You must hate me. I'm German." I let them know, because I didn't want to deceive them. Seeing the people, just bone and skin, and deadly sick, and having to carry many of them to the morgue. It was another bad experience.

The German soldiers in the hospital were moved out quickly, practically overnight. I don't know where they moved them to, but it didn't take long. They must have gone to another hospital, perhaps as prisoners of war. (My brother, as a wounded German soldier in France, was still there long after the war ended. He was discharged before he was able to travel.) Then all the concentration camp victims arrived.

There were quickly hundreds of them in the hospital, almost all Jews (there had been some German dissidents in the camp also). We had known they were coming; we were told ahead of time by the hospital authorities. They didn't call a meeting, they just told us individually. I asked what a concentration camp was, and they said it was a prison camp, and the prisoners were forced to work in factories, they were mistreated, and that it had been an extermination camp. The patients arriving were near death, having been starved.

The patients told how they didn't get any food, and they had to work. If someone got too weak, they just died or were killed. Some were so stunned they didn't even talk. They were so sick, you didn't even have conversations with them. They had typhus. They were starved. They were dehydrated. They had tuberculosis. They had digestive problems, many with diarrhea. We hadn't been trained in how to treat them. There wasn't much we could do; no intravenous was available. There was minimal medication available, but no antibiotics—later, when penicillin became available, though in short supply, physicians had to send an application to get permission.

Most of the patients died. We knew they weren't going to make it, and we were essentially just trying to keep them as comfortable as possible. Their temperature was up, so you gave them a lot of water and sponge-bathed them. Their temperature rose day by day, and they were so weak. They couldn't eat, and would bring up everything they tried to get down. You knew that eventually they would die. Every day when you came on, you knew that a bunch had died during the night, and their beds were immediately filled. Before they came in the hospital the first time, they were all de-loused, shaved from head to toe (to combat the lice) and bathed. The lice transmitted the typhus. There was infection control, but of course not as rigorous as it is today. You had to wash your hands. There were hardly any bandages, any gloves, any materials. Every bit of gauze had to be re-washed after use, sterilized (by boiling), and re-used again. You couldn't throw anything out; it all had to be re-used.

The staff had to examine each other every night, looking under collars and things to make sure we didn't have any lice. Some doctors and nurses got typhus from being infested with lice, and some died.

The Gunskirchen camp was perhaps ten kilometers from the hospital in Wels. There was a railway leading in, and the camp was fenced, so afterward people said they thought it might have been a munitions factory, or an ammunition dump. There was a sign that said *"Militärischer Gebiet. Geben Sie nicht."* (Military area. Do not enter.) I was shocked to see the patients. I had never seen anything like it. I was numb. I don't know how to describe it. I had no idea the camp had been there. We talked about it among the staff, and wondered how it could have happened.

Every day, people who had come from the concentration camp died, on every floor. On our floor, four or five could die in one day, out of maybe thirty patients. The local armory was full of people from the camps, and as many as could be accommodated were moved to the hospital. As people died in the hospital, their beds were filled by more people from the armory, until the armory was empty. Everybody who arrived was extremely sick, so there was no preference about who went first. There were other temporary places that housed patients waiting to get into the hospital, like houses that still had floors or rooms, or schools. Once the armory was empty, we started taking people from the temporary places. A few patients survived, but the majority were just skin and bone. We were so stunned by this. We never expected to face this. It's like happening upon the scene of a car accident, and seeing people mangled. You take it in, but you don't take in the severity until afterward. You became almost inured after a while. It wasn't that you didn't care; it was just that there were too many bad things.

By the time I left in November, most of the camp victims at the hospital had died, and local Austrians patients were gradually being brought in, such as returning Austrian soldiers.

Expulsion

During the war, there was no distinction between Germans and Austrians. When the war was finished in 1945, all of a sudden Germany was no friend of Austria. Then came the declaration that Austria was not part of Germany anymore. They were their own republic. This was when all Germans were dismissed, sent out of Austria. The Austrians demanded it, and the Americans didn't run the country.

A loudspeaker was driven through the streets—it was the only kind of communication, as radio and all those things, nothing was working yet. Every German with last names starting with 'A' through 'M' (or something like that) would have to assemble within two hours down at the city center for transport back to Germany. Just take with you what you can carry. They had to go, there was no choice. The Americans knew who they were. When anyone traveled those days from city to city, they had to sign out in the town they started from, and sign in where they stopped. They always knew where people were. I don't know of a case where someone didn't go. Everyone had passports to identify themselves. People didn't have much in the way of possessions. (For me, I didn't have much to begin with, anyway.)

I knew with my name I'd be next. I was working at a Catholic hospital, and I went right away to the Mother Superior, and told her it wouldn't be long until they called for 'N' through 'Z,' including my 'S' for Speidel. I told her I had no idea where to go. There had been no communication for a whole year—you couldn't write a letter, you couldn't phone, I didn't know where my older brother was (my other brother was killed). I didn't know that he was sent from the Russian front to the Western front and was badly wounded in the invasion. I found this all out afterward. I didn't know where my little sister was. I didn't know whether my grandmother still lived. I didn't know anything. I said, "Our house is destroyed, I have no home, nothing. I don't know where to go." I didn't know if any of my relatives in Germany were still alive, or, if they were, where they would be. There was no post office, so you couldn't send mail. You couldn't talk to anybody. Usually you would go your hometown, but I didn't know where I would have gone.

She said she would speak to the American commander, whose office was in the hospital. She personally got an extension for me to stay. Many others certainly had this same problem as me, but I was lucky to be working at that hospital, and to know the Mother Superior. I worried that if I went with the next shipment, I wouldn't know where to go. I hoped that I would be able to find out in the meantime if anyone was alive. I was afraid to go home, and I didn't want to leave the comfort of the hospital. I didn't know how long the extension would last, but it turned out to be for six months.

During the six months extension in Wels, there was no way to get any information about home. You still couldn't telephone, you couldn't write, you couldn't send mail, nothing. It was at least a year before there was postal service or anything like that. The telephone lines were not in service. Nothing worked. Travel was dangerous, and a normal two hour railway journey might take ten hours.

In November 1945, once again the Austrian government said all Germans, everybody, had to go home. There were no exceptions this time. I inquired with the Mother Superior again, but she said this time there was no choice; I had to go back. The extension she had originally got for me was finished.

We were told by loudspeaker, and the Mother Superior told us, too, that we had two hours. We could bring only what we could carry, though we didn't have much anyway. I had a battered leather suitcase with practically nothing it; maybe a few cigarettes. I had lost everything.

**

People didn't speak their opinion about whether the war was justified. I didn't either. I neither wished that Germany win the war nor lose it—I was neutral. Germany had occupied various countries, and would probably have occupied more if they could. You never knew what the end result would be—you'd just have to accept it. Even before Hitler committed suicide, we knew that the war was lost. You accepted what it was because you were sort of numb about the whole thing. It went on and on, and you wondered how long it would last but you didn't think about whether we would win or lose.

Looking back now, I know that the war was complete madness. It was not necessary at all. It was all because of that one crazy man (Hitler) who was power-seeking and wanted to rule the world. After the annexation of Austria shortly before his death, he said it would mean war, because it wasn't possible to just march into a country without any repercussions.

You didn't dare to talk with anyone about anything that was going on, whether you agreed or disagreed. You couldn't criticize anything, because you were so afraid that you or your family would get punished for it. People didn't express their opinions unless they knew each other really, really well.

Nobody knew what the future held for Germany. When the Nuremburg trials were on, most people said the Allies should have left the accused to the German people, because they would have killed them right away (without a trial, as they hadn't given anyone a chance at a trial). People remembered what happened after the First World War, and the effect of the Treaty of Versailles on Germany. The German character is not to capitulate, but to wait for an opportunity and start over again. Everyone was waiting to see what would happen with the end of this latest war, while recognizing that there was nothing they could do about it, regardless.

Each person was so busy with their own personal problems and worries that they didn't have time to think about larger issues. Some had come from what would become East Germany, and knew they wouldn't be able to go home because it had been taken over by the Russians. If they had gone home, they might have been detained there, and everybody knew how bad the Russians were. Some worried about their wives, or girlfriends, or children they'd never met.

The division of Germany had been a shock. It was part of the revenge against those who lost the war. Some common-sense people said it was just the price we had to pay for starting the war. Some people, like former Nazis, did not think it was right at all.

6. Consequences of War

1945 Stuttgart, Germany

Return Trip

I said goodbye to the nuns at the hospital, and I cried. Sister Angelica was still there. We hugged each other, and she said she would pray for me. We had gotten along so well, and it was so comfortable. It had been like home for me. Every hospital I went to, it was like home for me.

I went to the assembly place in the market square, and I was told to get on one of the trucks that were waiting. This particular one was a cattle truck, and it was going to Stuttgart. I don't know how many other trucks there were, but they had it sorted out so you got on a truck that was going near to your town. You had to show your identification; they had my name on their list. Off we went, and it took a good three or four days before we arrived in Stuttgart. I paid my own way.

There were around fifteen of us. November was cold. We sat on rough benches around the perimeter of the truck bed, and we had a bucket for a common toilet. There was no embarrassment—we were beyond that. Women would stand in front to provide a screen for other women. We helped each other, and everyone was discreet. There was no toilet paper, but there was newspaper. We had to get out in the middle of the night to walk, because the roads were full of bombing craters, and it was dangerous for the truck to maneuver around obstacles with people on it. We had to walk around, and meet when the road got level again.

There was a checkpoint at the border between Austria and Germany. We weren't questioned or anything. The driver just told them who we were and where we were going. He had his orders.

There wasn't much talking among the people riding in the back of the truck. We were depressed. Everybody was so stunned. It was such a blow. We were uprooted again, and we didn't know what the future would be. We couldn't even think about the future any more—we'd take whatever came. Our personal pride was a little hurt, because we had been told that we were the liberators, the master race, and now we weren't good enough to be there in Austria anymore. It wasn't that we thought before that we were better, but now we weren't respected. We were nothing. Before, they couldn't tell you to leave. We were just kicked out, and you couldn't go ask for help. The emotions were like a rollercoaster. It was a raw realization.

The truck stopped in Stuttgart, and everyone simply got off the truck. Nobody met us. We were just there.

The truck driver left to return to Austria.

Homeless

I was a refugee in my own country.

What little I had in Austria was lost. My shoes that I had originally gotten from the Red Cross had ended up with holes in them, so before I left I traded with a soldier for some military boots from the *Afrika Korps*. I gave him some trousers I had gotten from a pilot. I was left with my Red Cross coat, which wasn't warm, and some cigarettes. That's what I had, that's what I came home with to Germany.

Stuttgart itself was 90% destroyed, and a mess. The whole center was gone, where the railway station had been, and the kings' castle. Everything was demolished, with much debris. (European houses have a lot of stone and brick, with the only wood in the roof.

That's why it's so hard to get people out after earthquakes, with all the heavy debris like concrete.) Some streets were beginning to be cleared by the time I got there.

There was a large hill, now called *Scherbenhügel* (hill of shards). *Scherben* means shattered glass, broken things. It is a larger hill now, because rubble from the city was heaped on top there in the period after the war. Hundreds of people are buried there, since it was better to leave them buried than move them.

I had gone back to Stuttgart because that's where my school had been. I suppose I might have gone back to Ilshofen and my grandmother, but I had already left to do something, so I could not really go back.

The whole city was full of refugees, and I joined them. There were soldiers who returned home from duty or from prisoner of war camps, and there were people like me who'd been expelled from wherever they were. Those who had lived in the eastern parts of Germany couldn't go home, or didn't want to, because the Russians were there. There were people who had run away from the Russians, from Czechoslovakia, or whatever, and they hadn't had a bath in months and months. Most didn't know whether their families were alive

There were places you could ask for information. I inquired, and they told me that there was a refugee camp where you could sleep overnight, but only one night. I walked there (there were no streetcars or buses), because I had no other place to go. There were refugees from all over, and soldiers on their way home. They were all aimless, wandering around.

The next night, I was told there was another camp where I could sleep, so I went there. During the daytime, there was no opportunity to find out anything about anything — you couldn't travel, the roads weren't all clear, and there was no public transportation. One time I did hitchhike on a truck. I wanted to go outside Stuttgart, to a suburb, Cannstatt, since I once had an uncle living there. But I couldn't get there, I couldn't get through. There was no way I could get information about where my grandmother was, where my little sister was, who was still alive, where my oldest brother Hans was (I hadn't known he had ended up on the Western front).

Every night I slept in another refugee camp. Before you went in you had to be sprayed (de-loused). You slept with many other strangers, on big, big bunk beds with straw. I did this for about two weeks, with one meal a day, wandering from camp to camp. I sat in the canteen after lunch (not much — coffee, bread, turnip or powdered pea soup) talking with some ex-soldiers and other people. I still had my Red Cross uniform on, and when they saw me, they would talk about their problems, and weep. Some of them didn't know where their wives were, where their children were; some couldn't go back to where the Russians are, and things like that. They were still in their military uniforms, because there was nothing else. You still couldn't buy anything, and this is when the black market was running. We talked about our own miserable lives.

I listened to all the stories of troubles. I needed to be consoled, too. Sitting in that old uniform, I listened to them all day, and then I said to myself that I had to do something. I wanted to find a hospital, to find a job. I decided I would go from one hospital to the other looking for work. I thought since I had started out at the Red Cross, it was a way to get a roof over my head. I couldn't be aimless, not doing work. I would have regressed — you have to do something. You can't sleep every night in a different place. I wanted to live a normal life. A job would be my home, too, because if it was a hospital, I could stay in the residence there. I might as well as continue in a hospital, because that's what I could do.

Because I had arrived later than other Red Cross people, six months later, it was kind of a disadvantage for me. I went to hospital after hospital, and they said they couldn't take me on because they had to be accredited by the American health organization first, before they could take on students again. Germany had been divided in four by the conquering powers, and Stuttgart was in the American zone. The Americans closed every hospital nursing school, saying they had to be accredited first before they could reopen.

When the next night came, and I had to sleep somewhere else again, I thought I may as well take my life; there was just nothing else to it—just no way to continue. I was low; depressed; lonely; deserted; no goals; no sense of anything worth living for. I went to a bridge to jump into the Neckar River, but when I looked down I thought, "It's November. It's too cold to jump in there." I didn't hold onto that idea of suicide for long.

I went again to a Protestant (Lutheran) hospital run by Protestant sisters: *Karl-Olga Krankenhaus* (hospital). I found more sympathy this second time. The sister who met me (nurses were called 'sister,' although they weren't nuns, and they could have married, though most of them didn't) must have seen that I was desperate. I truthfully told her I'd go and take my life if I couldn't find work. Whether I would have been able to do it or not, I don't know, but I was desperate. She took the pages of references I'd brought, and disappeared to discuss things with her superior. It was about half an hour before she came back, and I knew this was a good sign. Oh, how I prayed. When she reappeared, she said, "Yes, we can take you. We'll take you as a nurses' aide for a few months until we've been accredited, and we can open our nursing school again, and then you can enroll into the nursing school." She asked where I was staying, and I told her about the camps, so she said I should come immediately.

Oh my goodness, but I was relieved. I would have a place to go, a place where I could do something. I had felt like a wandering nobody. It was more a sense of status then of duty. I felt like a wounded German, disillusioned about all the events. It had been difficult to get accepted at the hospital. You had always thought anything German would have been unquestionably successful. I was unbelievably relieved that they took me in—I felt a sense of pride again. I didn't feel as much alone. They were the only hospital that would take me. All the others wouldn't.

I slept in the residence there that night.

Karl-Olga

Karl-Olga was a civilian teaching hospital, a big general hospital. It was founded in 1894, and named in honor of the recently deceased King Karl (Charles) of Württemberg and his wife Queen Olga, a Russian. The hospital building had elevators, but not for people, only for transporting patients. We used the stairs. As a nurses' aide, I worked on a women's floor. I bathed the patients, made beds, things like that.

The hospital had an appealing garden around it. The buildings were still partially damaged from the war—perhaps one third of the hospital had been destroyed. It was modern for the time. There were balconies, where you could wheel the patients out in their beds.

There were physicians who were employed by the hospital, with the professor the number one physician ('professor' is the same word in German and English). The professor had his own practice, but he was in charge of the physicians and surgeons. When the professor came in the morning, there was always a meeting with his staff, with the doctors. There was a box on the ceiling in the corridor. There were different colored lights on it, and whoever ran the switchboard looked after it. When you wanted a doctor, his specific colored light would be switched on, so he would know he was being called. When the professor came, all of the lights came on, so you knew he was there and wanted to see all the doctors. That's how modern they were already, in the mid-forties.

Because the hospital had been bombed, many of the doctors who worked there lived there. We shared a wing, the doctors on one side and us on the other. All the doctors were male, and all the nursing staff was female. Later on, doctors and nurses both got their own residences again.

The hospital was well-supplied, although things like antibiotics were still scarce. The medical manufacturers in Germany had to start all over again. I remember one patient who had meningitis, and he was treated with streptomycin. The professor had to submit a requisition to the authorities, and state the condition of the patient. Only then, if they surrendered the antibiotic, could you treat the patient. If the antibiotics were scarce, you couldn't. This particular patient was saved, because we were able to get enough antibiotic.

One surgical patient had been an air force pilot during the war. Before his bombing missions, he loaded himself up with morphine to give him courage. He was still a drug addict and every hour he wanted morphine. One time, I told him it was too soon, and he threw a shoe at me. I knew he was just desperate.

We had many ex-soldiers as patients. Some of them had reconstructions of their stumps, where they had amputations. A lot of nurses found husbands from the soldiers who came for reconstructive surgery.

Food was slowly getting better, with more variety. It was becoming more typically German, with more vegetables, and things like meat, sausages and cheese. We ate all our meals at the hospital. We worked 12 hour shifts, with two hours in the afternoon for a rest. You went from seven to seven. After the mid-day meal, you slept most of the time, until it was time to go back to the ward again.

We got butter, because we nurses were considered to be 'heavy workers.' I didn't like the butter, and I traded it with patients for cigarettes. I smoked less than a pack a day (maybe twelve).

We often had root soup, sometimes for breakfast. We got two slices of bread a day. One day the soup was just too awful, and we sent it back. They said the Americans had given them some brown butter, a whole pail-full. ('Butter,' by the way, is spelled the same way in German and English, but it's pronounced with one difference—the Germans pronounce the first syllable of 'butter' similarly to the English pronunciation of 'boot.') The kitchen staff thought it would reinforce the soup a bit, to give us strength, so they put it in. It happened to be peanut butter. Nobody had told them what to do with it, because it's a North American food—even in England they didn't know about peanut butter. We couldn't eat it, and I don't know what they did with the rest of it. From that moment on, I hated peanut butter. I was in Canada for ten years before I accidentally ate it, and since then I've liked it.

It was around this time that I first saw nylon stockings. Only girlfriends of Americans had them. We talked this over among ourselves, and wondered how we could get nylons. One of my girlfriends said the only way was to find an American soldier and become his girlfriend. There were lots of American soldiers around, and some of them married German girls.

Once the streetcars began running, they were the only thing that had electricity all the time. For people's homes, there might be electricity from seven to nine, and from eleven to two, and from five to seven. People could cook before they left for work, and when they got home from work. The electricity supply system was for the most part destroyed, and what was left was restricted for many years.

After about three months working as a nurses' aide, in February 1946 I enrolled in Karl-Olga Hospital nursing school. They credited me for one year training for the time I did at the Red Cross, and I had to do two more years. I ended up being able to graduate in September 1947.

We had to work on the different hospital floors as the practical part of nursing school, but there was classroom work, too. When I graduated, I was a full nurse, a 'sister.' There wasn't convocation, as such. On the last day, we got together, and one of the professors of surgery at the hospital came and spoke to us. He told us to go out and use what we learned, but not to think that we knew it all. There was coffee and cake, and a few speeches, and then we left. None of my family came.

It was more fun once I finished school, and I loved what I was doing. One of the professors talked to us, and said that even though we were finished, not to think that meant we knew everything. He reminded us about Socrates, who had said, "I know nothing except the fact of my ignorance." That deflated us a bit.

My mood was good. I loved it there. I tried hard to do a good job, to be accepted. I wanted to be liked, but I enjoyed what I was doing. I put my whole heart into my work, and I always got good references. It was my home.

Post-War Living

Karl-Olga Hospital was not far from the boarding school I had gone to in Stuttgart during the war, maybe two blocks. I didn't go see it right away—I didn't want to. I knew the school had been largely destroyed during the war. I went to see it with my niece a few years ago, and it was still in ruins, though there were plans to redevelop it. It was one of the things gone with the war. You took things in stride, because you heard of this and of that being gone; so many things. It was just constant repetition.

There were so many emotions, so many events, that you couldn't cope with it all.

Some people committed suicide, especially after finding things out like their husband hadn't come back from the war, or had been killed. People in the canteen were pessimistic: How could we have lost the war? What about all the damage? Who is going to rebuild? What is the future?

Everybody was angry, surprised and upset about Hitler: How could he do that? How could we have believed in him? He deceived us. Why did he keep on fighting instead of giving up, when he knew we were losing the war? Why did so many people get killed? What do we have now? We had been told Hitler was a hero, someone we had to respect and worship; he was always right and could not fail; he was an exemplary leader. Now he was despised, and of course some people had never liked him to begin with.

We were stunned. The 'hero' was no hero anymore, but instead a disappointment.

We started to find out about things that were going on, like the Nuremburg war criminal trials. I thought it must have been quite a change for them, from high glory to being a prisoner, and being told what to do, with no more control over other people or themselves. We thought they deserved what they got, and that the outcome should have been left to the Germans. The Nazis never gave us a fair trial. When we heard what they were doing through the paper and the news, how they exterminated the Jews and the Gypsies, and how they looted things—this all came out afterward—it was one thing after another. You didn't agree with those principles. More fallen 'heroes.' They did wrong things, bad things. They weren't as good as we had thought they were.

There were people who knew more about the war than others. After the war, my little sister told me my grandmother had made a hole in a wall in her house, and hid a radio in there, covered with wallpaper. (She was somehow able to control it through the wallpaper.) She listened by putting her ear close to the wall. Having radios wasn't allowed, of course. She got the news in German from Radio Beromünster, which was in Switzerland. Switzerland got all the news form England. If she had been found out, she could have been killed for it. She heard all the news, and for example knew about what happened at Stalingrad in 1942 long before the German people heard about it officially. She had a cleaning lady, Mrs. Fischer, who was expecting twins, and it was a rule that a husband soldier who was in the war could get furlough for the birth of his child. The husband came, and it so happened that it came time for him to go back, but before the babies had arrived. So Mrs. Fischer went to my grandmother, and asked her what they could do. My grandmother phoned (she was one of the few people with a telephone) the Stuttgart headquarters and spoke to the commandant. The conversation was like this. She phoned, and she told whoever answered that there was no point in her speaking with them, she wanted to speak to the commandant. She didn't give up, and eventually got to speak to the commandant. He must have said to her, "Do you know that there is a war going on?" She said, "Yes, I know there is a war going on, and furthermore I will tell you that we have lost the war already." That was after Stalingrad. The officer didn't say anything, because he probably knew himself. She continued, "If they have twin boys, that gives more cannon fodder for Hitler." She got the extension, and the babies came. They were triplets, and all three were girls. That was my grandmother.

Every once in a while during the war, every month or so, she would go by train to Heilbronn (it was only four or five stops from Ilshofen, where she lived). It was a big city, the one where my father was born. She went to visit the *Hotel Vaterland* (Fatherland Hotel), which was right opposite the railway station there. The owner, a lady, sometimes said to me if I happened to be with my grandmother, "If I had married your father, you could be my daughter now." (Apparently, she had been a one-time girlfriend of my father.) The contact was kept up with my grandmother. They had a *Papagei* (parrot) in the lobby that talked, and they had a son whose name was Hugo. The parrot would always say, "*Hugo, wo bist du?*" (Hugo, where are you?). It was quite an attraction. We didn't know why my grandmother went there, but we found out after the war that she would meet some of her first husband's friends, who were retired military officers. She would tell them all the war news she had heard on the radio from Switzerland. Nobody else knew what was really going on with her meetings; they thought they were just meeting socially. My sister somehow found out, though, and my grandmother told her, "If you tell anybody, I'll have to kill you!" (Don't worry, my sister didn't tell me about it until long after the war.)

The American and British occupation forces were immediately liked. The Russians weren't liked because the Russians were cruel and did terrible things. We never thought they were nice. The Russians hated the Germans, and vice versa. There was always a little bit of things with the French, but there always had been. The danger was out of the way. If you met an American, it was just another human being. You didn't make a judgment like, "Oh, I shouldn't talk to him, he's my enemy."

After the war, you could say anything about the past. It was common to talk about the Russians, because the problems associated with them were well known. There was no fear of saying the wrong thing, or being persecuted for saying something.

* * *

Everybody knew about the black market. Everybody knew where to go if they were looking for something. It was a known thing, but it wasn't stopped because there was no infrastructure yet. The stores didn't have much. As soon as the money changed, the stores had merchandise you could buy. If you had cigarettes, you could buy things, even cars.

You might have had money, but it didn't matter because there was nothing to buy. I had come back from Austria with my *Afrika Korps* boots, which were high, above the ankle. The upper part wasn't leather, but made of a fine woven material up to the knee to keep the sand out. They were men's boots, and I had to get rid of them, as they weren't feminine. I had nothing else. Slowly, you got out of your old slump, and tried to improve your life and everything that goes with it. I needed boots. I was told there were Jewish people who survived the concentration camps somehow. There were Jews who lived in Russia before the war, but Jews were not always liked there. They had gotten away to Germany. We heard that in Stuttgart there was a particular street where there were Jewish people selling shoes, and on another street, selling hats. I don't know where they got the merchandise from, but you'd go and say you needed a particular shoe size. They would leave you on the street, and go back into their empty bombed-out houses (or wherever they had their supply) and bring out five different styles of shoes, but only one of each pair. You tried them on, and if they fit and you liked them, they went back inside and brought out the second one, and then you paid, maybe 50 of the old *reichsmarks*. I just left my old boots there, though maybe I should have kept them as a memento. Unfortunately, I would have had no place to store them.

After my parents died 1938, my oldest brother was the executor. However, the money was handled by the notary. We didn't know how much money we had, because it was divided among us four children. I couldn't believe it, because money was never a problem. When my brother died, was killed, it was divided among we three.

Because of the war, I lost out on going to university. We had the money, and I would have gone, but of course I wasn't able to. After the war ended, we still had money in the bank, maybe 40,000 marks each. It was soon devalued. In the late forties, Germany couldn't compete in the world market, and the currency was changed (about 1948) because it had no value. All your savings were gone. Again it was announced over loudspeakers, "Bring all your cash to the banks—the notes will be burned and the coins will be melted down." All your savings were gone, valueless. Everybody got 40 new German marks that first week, whether you were the head of the government or a street sweeper. One week later, when payday came, you'd get paid according to your position. Germany, with the new currency, was starting to build up again, and compete in the world market. We, like many, many other Germans, lost everything.

I bought a pair of leather gloves with the 40 marks, and then the 40 marks were gone. The black market stopped after that.

※ ※ ※

The Stuttgart opera house had been mostly destroyed, but the Americans still used it in the evenings for their entertainment, and the Germans used it in the daytime for opera. Somehow, it kept us going. There was a young doctor who worked at the hospital, first name Hans, who didn't have much money, either. I happened to see him at the opera once, and it turned out he liked the opera too, although he didn't have much money. After that, we often went to the opera together, though we were not romantically involved. I worked specifically night shifts, eight in the evening to eight in the morning. I went to the ticket office on Monday mornings at ten, and I got tickets for opera for the week. Most of the time, I paid for his ticket, too.

I went to an opera performance right after the currency change (I had the tickets from beforehand), to see 'Orpheus in the Underworld;' there were only eight people there. They had paid with their new money. Things had changed. No one else had spent their money on opera tickets. There was a high school nearby, and they sent somebody there to ask if the students could come to the opera, so the cast didn't have to perform in front of an empty house. They asked us all to sit in the front seats.

❋ ❋ ❋

The people were proud of their soldiers, because the German soldier was a good soldier. They felt sorry for them. They had learned to fight, but for nothing. People hardly talked about it, though.

We knew the difference between the SS and the regular army. The regular army was fair, and was respected. With the SS, sometimes there was no choice—they had just been involuntarily enrolled. But some had chosen to join, the rebellious types. They like to have power to hurt people, to have people under them, and hurt them. People didn't like the SS, because they were a danger. Some of the SS would have been willing to kill their own parents. They had to swear with their life not to tell what they were doing.

For the ex-soldiers who didn't have a home to go to, or a city to go to, there was always someone to help them—a neighbor, for example. They also opened agencies where people could go. The Red Cross had a radio station, with announcements every day like, "Today a soldier by the name of so-and-so came someplace, and the last time December 20 he saw a soldier by the name of Georg from so-and-so city. If anybody knows him, please notify us or telephone us." So, somebody looking for their son might hear this, and know that he was still alive. I lost two cousins, children of my uncle in Cannstatt—they disappeared during the war. Both had started first-year university. Every day, the aunt listened to the radio of the Red Cross station, where they announced the name of the soldiers who had returned, and where his home was. This is how they got connections. But her sons were never mentioned. The Red Cross had established a line where you could report someone you were looking for, what their name was. Every city had one, and they'd let each other know. "We have a man here by the name of _____; he comes from your city."

I sometimes wonder if my two cousins were on the Russian front, and were transferred to the Western Front on that train that went through Wels and was bombed on Christmas. Who knows? There is no trace of them.

I was relieved that the war was over. I had a job, and I had gotten back on my feet. Everyone was relieved Germans were busy people—they didn't give up. You knew you had to help yourself, and that things would improve. And they did—slowly, slowly, they improved. At first, time seemed to have stopped for a while, but then living conditions got better. The economy improved. Streetcars were running more often. Once the money changed, there were things in the stores. Sometimes you traded with people. Sometimes you'd go out to the trade with farmers. Now the farmers could do what they wanted with their produce, so people would go out with something to trade, say for eggs. The Americans were still there, and their military police. I remember in the Stuttgart railway station when people would come with all their produce from the farms, and the military police took it away from the Germans. The trains were running again after the war, and they went out to the farms to trade things for food. Food was still not plentiful. They came back with bread and eggs, and the MPs would check everyone's hand luggage as soon as they arrived, and took everything away from them. They said they were hoarding food illegally. I didn't have to do things like that, because I had food at the hospital. Those people went home without anything. It's human nature for people to do things they think they can get away with.

Post-War Family

At the end of the war, my little sister Liselotte was living with one of my father's sisters, but in another town—she was just ten years old when the war ended. Later, she was sent to boarding school.

I never had much family life with my sister, due to circumstances that were out of my control. When I came back from Austria after the war, I did not know at first where my sister was living—was she still alive? Did she survive the war? It's difficult to imagine a country as in ruin as Germany was after the war, with no transportation and no telephone system. It took several months before I found out, through an uncle who lived near Stuttgart, that she was with my grandmother, who was also alive. By then I was employed at the hospital. Our reunion with my sister and grandmother was like establishing a relationship all over again. For me it was bittersweet. I loved Liselotte, but we felt like strangers. I felt profoundly sorry and sad that this sweet person had less family love than I had, and that I could not give it to her. My love for her grew stronger, but again since I was working in another town, we did not see each other as much as we would have liked.

By that time we didn't have any money, so she couldn't go to university, either. She worked for a time as a secretary transcribing physicians' reports in a Protestant Hospital called *Diakonissen Haus* (Deaconess House) in Schwäbisch Hall. Later, she worked as a secretary at a brewery in the same town. She met her future husband there, Josef Rollny, who was a Catholic. They were married in 1958, with Liselotte having converted to Catholicism the year before. They had three children, two girls and one boy Liselotte's husband was a district administrator for Kraft Foods, and travelled around visiting stores that stocked their products. He died in 1978 of a sudden heart attack, at age 48. It was New Year's Day, they came home from a party, and he dropped dead. They started to build a house in Ellhofen, but they never saw it finished. A year and a half later, my sister died of a brain tumor. She was 44.

My brother Hans was first in Russia during the war, and then was moved to help defend the Normandy invasion. He was taken as a prisoner of war, and was in a hospital in France until three months after the war. He needed skin grafts while he was there. After he was released, he stayed with my little sister for a while. He came to see me in Stuttgart; at our reunion we fell into each other's arms, lost for words.

He needed money for school, and construction in those days was a big industry, so he started there once he was strong enough. It paid well. With the money he made, he put himself through University of Stuttgart, graduating with a degree in architecture. He married a Catholic woman, Maja, while he was still a student, but he did not become a Catholic. They had one son, Hans Peter, who was baptized a Catholic and was for many years an altar boy.

I sometimes talked with my sister about the Catholic faith, but not with my brother. He was closed up about everything. I tried to ask him several questions, but he just didn't want to talk about things. He lived in Crailsheim, working there as an architect and eventually as an investigator for courts in cases concerning architecture. He died there in 2003.

In my family tree, which a relative has traced back to 1356, there was a Catholic Archbishop of Vienna in the 1600s. Way back there must have been Catholics amongst my ancestors.

I had gone to Catholic services at the hospital in Wels. I felt some air of "lifting up," somehow. I felt that because of the nuns, and their atmosphere in the hospital. It was spiritual, but I didn't yet know it was spiritual. The Mother Superior and Sister Angelica were my spiritual mentors. When I had problems, I went to them, and they'd invite me to pray. I said I believed my parents were protecting me, and they'd say yes, they were acting as my guardian angels.

I just soaked up the atmosphere at mass. I remember the nuns singing hymns, such as *Nun danket alle Gott* (Now Thank We All Our God). I particularly liked the Christmas midnight mass, and all the singing. I tried to go every Sunday, but sometimes there wasn't time because we worked such long hours. My faith evolved more after I got to Canada.

I always sat at the front at church. Whenever I went walking with my parents, I always was in front. Whenever I go on tours now, whenever I travel, I always walk in front. It's tiring to walk behind other people. It's better to have a steady gait, than walking slowly behind people. I always go in front.

My relationship with God wasn't well-developed yet. I went to church, sometimes even when there wasn't a service. Sometimes I just liked to look at the architecture of the churches, too. We had prayers sometimes at the hospital with the Protestant sisters (nurses), where there were always lovely surroundings.

Graduation

My mother had been in a Catholic hospital for long periods. With their long, flowing habits, the nun nurses impressed me with how they seemed to be literally sailing through the air without walking. I thought: I'll become a nurse. It probably wouldn't have happened if my parents hadn't died when they did, or there had been no war.

At the hospital nursing school, we were taught by doctors. We had mostly oral exams. It wasn't really difficult—it was more difficult later in Canada, in English.

I was hired automatically by the hospital after I graduated. The administration decided to send me to a sister hospital, in Heidenheim, which had requested help there. They wanted me to get experience in orthopedics, although the understanding was that I could be recalled to Stuttgart at any time.

1947 Heidenheim, Germany

The name of the hospital in Heidenheim was *Kreiskrankenhaus* (district hospital). It was not formally a teaching hospital, and I ended up affiliating in obstetrics. It was a train trip of about an hour and a half to there from Stuttgart, almost due east. I was happy to go. When I left the hospital in Stuttgart in the autumn of 1947, they had said, "Just go, and do whatever they tell you."

Heidenheim was also in the American sector. Once Germany was divided, you knew which sector you'd end up in, and you had to accept it. I took everything in stride. I don't know if I became insensitive, or if I just accepted it. I was just a little drop in the ocean, so I may as well just go with the stream of the tide, and not let it upset me.

I lived in a house on the hospital grounds. Why would you want to pay rent to go somewhere else when it was all free? It was all lovely, too; beautiful. It was a private home, with various rooms and several stories. You had a bed, chairs and a desk in your own room—the furniture was provided, but you could bring in whatever you wanted. The food was good. There was still a little bit of shortage of food, but it got better and better. Slowly, we began to get imported food again, like oranges and bananas.

Our family food had been unusual when I was a child, because of my father's illness: not much meat, and lots of fruit and vegetables. He would get fresh pineapple, bananas and oranges from Spain. Breakfast in Germany had never been bacon and eggs, until the Americans arrived. You'd have fresh bread, or buns, and jam—plum, strawberry, raspberry, a lot of it homemade. When you could first buy jam in the store, nobody liked it, but later when there were shortages you'd be happy to get it. There'd be coffee, although children never got real coffee, but instant a hot chicory drink. My father had mocha, to give him a little bit of energy. Mocha is a strong coffee, which is made by boiling it over and over. If you're not used to it, it drives your heartbeat up like nothing else. Lunch was always the main meal.

At the hospital, breakfast was usually early, about seven o'clock. We always stopped for lunch at noon, and we had a two hour rest after the meal was finished. There was meat (pork, chicken or beef, but cooked in different ways), vegetables, potatoes or noodles. We would drink mostly juice, usually apple. You never drank water — it didn't taste good. At two o'clock, you went back to work again. We had coffee breaks in the morning and afternoon, where you could have tea or juice, too. There would be leftover desserts, too, like cake. Supper would be at about six o'clock. We often had rösti (a fried potato dish), sometimes even with fresh cherries. There was no dessert as such; maybe some fruit. Every evening, we had an apple.

I had dates in Heidenheim, but I wasn't thinking about marriage yet. There was an unmarried female patient, and her married sister had a son, Walter. They practically adopted me into the family, and the son and I were a little bit romantically involved. Nothing became of it, but on my days off they wanted me to visit, and on Sundays they would come to the hospital and visit me, and bring me treats like cake.

For dates then, you'd go to movies, to dances. Sometimes you'd go to a wine pub, and somebody would sit down at a piano and play, and someone else would get up to dance, and then you would dance, and before you knew it, everybody would be dancing. It wasn't organized most of the time, but there were things like New Year's dances. We danced mostly waltzes. I had learned to dance when I was at boarding school. You'd dance with many people, not just one partner. You might have a glass of wine, or wine mixed with water. You usually went as a group, instead of just one pair. There were sometimes blind dates offered to me, but I didn't like them. I was picky.

For my nursing work, they would assign you to a patient in the morning. You'd help them bath, and make the bed and sometimes you were assigned to give medication. You just started, and eventually get to know the routine. The nursing is similar in all countries — the need of the patients is the purpose.

Early in the autumn of 1949, I was told that I was being sent to a new position at an associated hospital. It was in a town called Neuenbürg in the *Schwarzwald* (Black Forest), 60 kilometers or so west of Stuttgart. I had to go practically the next day.

I've never met a bad person who could drag me down. I've met lots of good people, people who took me in their home. In Heidenheim (where Rommel was born) and Neuenbürg, I stayed in houses with good people. In Heidenheim, there was a married couple, and they took me in. Every weekend, they wanted me to go spend time with them. People always were nice. God was good to me, such as when I met my two nice husbands.

1949 Neuenbürg, Germany

The Hospital

When I arrived by train in Neuenbürg, some of my new colleagues from the hospital came and met me at the station that night. We had to walk up, up, up a hill, because the hospital was on the top of a hill, overlooking the forest and the surrounding valley. It is picturesque. There are natural wells in the ground there, and there are many spas.

We made it to the hospital, and the food they served that night was potatoes and smoked herring, which I love. Electricity was still rationed, and there was no electric light at the hospital in the evening, just candles. (It took years to get the entire infrastructure built up again.) The smoked herring was full of bones, and in the candlelight, I had to be careful to not get any bones stuck in my throat. I survived this meal, but, oh, how I remember how hard it was to eat that herring in the dark, with all its little bones.

The *Krankenhaus Neuenbürg* was a district hospital. There were no students there, only professional nurses who had graduated. It was on the top of the hill, above the town. It was lovely, surrounded by beautiful countryside. It was a Protestant (Lutheran) hospital, and the sisters held prayers in the morning, before breakfast, although they didn't take very long. I wasn't so connected with God or religion; it was just part of the daily ritual. I hadn't really 'woken up' yet; the breaking-point of awareness would come later.

I worked on the medical floor and the surgical floor. I had good rapport with the patients and staff—I felt competent in my nursing duties, and I got more responsibility as time went on. I was happy in Neuenbürg, and I liked what I was doing. It was a pleasant area, a pleasant hospital and a friendly place. It quickly became my home. I wouldn't have wanted to stay forever, though, as I always eventually got wanderlust.

There was no hospital residence, because there were no student nurses. Instead, the hospital rented rooms for us in private houses, and I had a single room, in a house that was just a few hundred meters away from the hospital. It was an old couple who lived there, and our bedrooms were on the same floor. When I arrived home from work, it was usually late, and I went into their bedroom to visit with them. That's how much at home I felt there. They always wanted to talk with me, so we would chat while they lay in bed (like a Grandpa and Grandma) and then I went to bed. I would have to get up at six o'clock the next day. There was no electric or central heat; instead there was a wood-burning stove in each room. By the time I got home, I was always too tired to get the stove started, so when they went to bed, they would move their metal *Bettflasche* (hot water bottle) into my bed. When I went to bed, I had a warm bed.

Upstairs in that same house lived a couple, a lawyer and his wife. They had escaped from the Russian sector, but before they left, his wife delivered a baby in the presence of Russian soldiers. The soldiers kept the husband at gunpoint while they raped the wife after the birth of the baby. She was sick, and infected, afterward. She could not have children again. This was the type of thing the Russians did. A lot of women had abortions in Heidenheim, and elsewhere, because they were raped by Russian soldiers.

※ ※ ※

The Black Forest is full of wild blueberries, and when they were in season, we would go into the forest to collect them. At that time, the Black Forest was also full of wild hogs. During the war, the boars had been driven into the forest from France ahead of the Allied armies advancing west. There were an unusually large number of them, and there was always the danger of being run into. Many people had been injured by them, so you would have to go in pairs, or threes. As Germany built up again, as more roads and buildings were constructed, the hogs were driven elsewhere. It was an unusual thing.

We worked long hours, with twelve-hour shifts. It wasn't unusual to work extra hours, as well. In those days there was no recovery room, so if you were on a surgical floor, after your patient came out of surgery you stayed with him until he was stable.

With what spare time there was, we would go to the nearest large town, which was Pforzheim, about ten kilometers north. It was industrial; they made jewelry there. We would look around, do shopping, and go to concerts or movies.

We didn't do formal physical exercise. There wasn't time—we worked six and a half days a week. Being in the Black Forest, it was a skiing area. The weather was predictable, and there was a lot of snow in the winter. It was never too hot in the summer, as it was atop a hill and in a forest. If it was humid, I didn't notice it, but in those days before air conditioning, you could just open a window if it was needed.

Tadeusz

Tadeusz Kurowski (pronounced *tah-deh'-oosh kur-ov'-ski*) was a patient in the hospital, and in fact he was my patient. He had gallstones, and he was in a private room. He told me that he was with the IRO, the International Refugee Organization, under the auspices of the United Nations. Germany was flooded with refugees. Entire subdivisions would be devoted to refugees. If a particular house had six rooms, then six refugee families would be moved in there. They would eventually emigrate, but it took years to get all their papers together. He was in charge of getting all the refugees in the district through the emigration process.

He was a real gentleman. When I went in and introduced myself, right away we had a rapport—the chemistry worked. Although Neuenbürg was in the French occupation zone, he received American rations, and every afternoon at four o'clock he invited another nurse and me for coffee in his room. It was nice. You know how things go. Even though there was an age difference (he was 15 years older than me), I could relate to him. I was never happy with someone my own age, because they were never mature enough. I was happy with him—we connected. Maybe I was looking for a father figure. Slowly, slowly, it grew, that we liked each other. However, his wife was still alive (which I knew) so he never let on, even though I knew that he liked me. He had a house in Neuenbürg, and a chauffeur. The chauffeur would come and pick him up every morning and drive him to embassies and consulates in various cities.

He brought me good food, from the Americans. He knew I liked sardines. So on a Sunday (after he'd been released), he came to the hospital and brought sardines for me and the other nurses. He would bring candies that he had gotten from the Americans to children in the hospital, too.

Tadeusz's wife, Jakubina (Jacqueline), was in Poland. She had breast cancer. Under the Russians, they didn't have easy access to medication. He couldn't get her out, and he couldn't go back because he would have been imprisoned since he had been part of the pre-war Polish government—Poland was then under Russian occupation. He had married her before the war. The only people they let out to go to the west were old people. Tadeusz and his brother were adamant that they did not join the fight with the Allies to establish a communist dictatorship in their own country.

He sent money and medicine to her through a Polish trading post called Pekao. You could pay with American money, and the money or goods would be delivered to Poland. He also sent money for his son to get through university. The son eventually came to visit him in Canada, and also the grandson.

I had no problem connecting with Tadeusz, who was older than I was. We got along splendidly, and age didn't mean anything. He was a good influence on me; very good. In every way—in outlook, in respect, in prestige, in everything. We talked about God. My embracing of Catholicism was born in Austria, with the nuns, but it had slumbered for a while. He brought it out again—how he lived; his principles. This was the breaking point, where it grew. Before then, when people were nasty, I couldn't forgive them. After meeting Tadeusz, I could forgive anybody, anything. To this day, I can forgive anybody, anything.

Every Sunday he went to mass, even if he had been up until six o'clock in the morning. He was such an example. He said one hour a week was not too much to ask of us, considering what God gives us. He didn't force me to go to mass. He didn't say, "Go!" He didn't push me. He just waited. By his example, my faith came to me. I knew there was something. During the war, a lot of people had said to me things like, "How could there be a God? He allowed this. He allowed that. My husband got killed. That woman got killed." I couldn't dispute it, because I didn't know whether God had allowed it. But I knew flowers couldn't grow without something from above.

Tadeusz's faith was strong—unbending. I told him how obvious it was that he loved his mother. He said, no, he loved God, and then came his mother. His faith never broke, ever. It always kept him and his brother on top of everything. When they were in a prison camp during the war, they had a chapel, and they had the Catholic mass there. (There were priests who were also prisoners in the camp.) The mass was held in French and in Polish. His religion was unbending.

He had a little pocket book of prayers, and after we got married, he knelt beside the bed every night and prayed his little pocketbook of prayers. His mother had given this little Polish prayer book to him when he joined the army. It had prayers for all occasions. He said the rosary every time he prayed, too. When I met him in the hospital, he asked for a priest to come visit him. I was impressed by this. I was reminded of when I was still in Austria, and I saw the Americans come Sunday for mass, how impressive it was that they went to church. It was a complete turnaround; there was obviously something more to life than just misery, killing and hate.

It was a pleasant shock back into reality, that people can go to church in spite of everything that had happened. I was inspired by their faith and desire. So I joined them at the mass. From then on, my seeds were slowly growing to become Catholic.

His brother, Władysław (pronounced *vlah-dee-swahv*, Walter in English and German), was a physician for refugees. He worked in a hospital in another spa town in the Black Forest, Villingen, which was about 100 kilometers south of Neuenbürg. He came visiting; both brothers were devoted Catholics. Władysław was a perfect gentleman in perpetuity, and very kind. He was a person you could confide in easily.

Władysław's girlfriend, Ursula, was a German from Berlin. She escaped with her mother after her father starved to death under the Russian occupation. Food was scarce, and she and her parents were often hungry and had diarrhea from malnutrition. At night they went out and stole potatoes from where people had gardens on rented land. One day they ate the potatoes, and the next day they ate the skins because they had nothing else to eat. They decided to leave, hiding during the day, and walking toward the west at night. They made it. If they had been caught by the Russians, they would have been not only raped but also likely murdered. By the time I met her and the Kurowskis at Neuenbürg in 1947, they had already been a year or so in West Germany. She worked as a nurse, and she and Władysław were married before they left for Canada in 1950. There was an age difference with them, too, for some reason.

Władysław's mother-in-law moved from Berlin to live with them for a while, and did their cooking. The larger the family, the more ration cards you got. So, with four people, there could get at least one roast a week. They invited me on Sundays, and shared it with me.

The Kurowski Brothers

Tadeusz Kurowski was born in Warsaw, in Poland, March 10, 1910. He studied agriculture, agronomy (the science of agriculture) and biology there at the University of Warsaw. His brother's degree was in medicine. Neither was allowed to speak Polish at university, because of pressure from Russia; they could speak Polish only at home during those years. After graduation, he worked with the Polish ministry of agriculture in Warsaw. He was involved in experiments with husbandry, artificial insemination of cattle, and he was responsible for dairy export to England—butter, for example.

Before the war started, his parents built a big house in the country, outside Warsaw—that's where Tadeusz's grandson still lives. It had eleven rooms. They had a little pond with fish, and they raised horses. The brothers spent their summers out there, with a lot of land around, and away from the main highway.

When the Germans came, they had to leave the city (by then their father had died), and there were left only the brothers, their mother, her maid and a helper-gardener. They all moved out to this place, and this is where their mother spent the rest of her life. The Germans left it alone, and eventually the Russians left it alone, too. The Germans did move into their house in Warsaw, where they had four underground garages. They were wealthy people. His father was in import and export, mainly with wheat.

When Germany attacked Poland in September of 1939, Tadeusz joined the military. Poland's so-called friends, the Russians, never came to their aid. They waited until Poland was crushed by the Germans, before eventually helping themselves to half of Poland. But they never helped Poland.

When they realized the war was lost, Tadeusz's unit didn't want to be captured by the Germans and end up as prisoners of war. They didn't want to go to the Russians, because they hated the Russians. The Russians always had an influence on Poland. Poland is an unfortunate geographic situation—the Germans on one side, and the Russians on the other. They decided that their unit and the whole military headquarters were better just to leave, to escape. It was 'five minutes to twelve,' and they knew they had better leave the country.

Before leaving Poland, the whole group with which Tadeusz escaped (hundreds of people) needed visas to be able to pass through the various countries on their route out. With just one civilian jacket available among all of them, they passed it from one man to the next as they had their individual photographs taken, all wearing the same jacket, so they would not be labeled as military. They escaped with the military headquarters through Romania and Italy, to the south of France, close to the Pyrénées. He ended up joining a Polish division of the Free French army, but he didn't want to be an officer, just a private in the infantry. Working as an interpreter, he was surprised to see members of the French military wearing white gloves.

He was taken prisoner during fighting in France, sometime in 1940. He was brought to Strasbourg, in eastern France, and held prisoner in a fortress there. Tadeusz said it wasn't good—the food was not good, and it was scarce. He was fortunate that his parents were interested in making sure that their two sons learned a lot of languages. For three years when he was a child, they had a German teacher from Berlin, and every day they spoke in German. They had three years with a teacher from the Sorbonne, and every day was spoken French. He was fluent—reading, writing and speaking—in Polish and those two languages, plus he could speak Russian, some Ukrainian, Latin and eventually English. He spoke German with the German soldiers who took him prisoner. They said, "You must be a German." He said, "No, I'm Polish." He spoke so many languages, that they made him the interpreter in the prison camp. Tadeusz said he would become the interpreter for the camp only if they asked all 3,000 prisoners if they agreed with it. If they didn't agree with it, he wouldn't be the interpreter. There was a vote, and he was appointed as the interpreter for the entire time of his imprisonment.

From Strasbourg, he was sent to another prisoner of war camp run by the regular German army, near Villingen in Germany (likely *Stalag* 5B). About twenty kilometers away was a prison camp run by the SS, and Tadeusz knew that if he had been in a camp run by them, it would have been awful. The SS was Hitler's personal army, and they were trained to be cruel. They didn't have to follow orders of regular army officers, even of Rommel, as I mentioned earlier. They were an entirely different organization.

His brother was taken prisoner near Danzig (Gdansk in Polish), after Tadeusz had left the country. Władysław had been fighting in the Polish army. Their mother sent Tadeusz food from Poland to the prison camp, and he found out from her that his brother was a prisoner in Danzig. The German government recognized the Geneva Conventions (although the Japanese didn't), and one of its directives was that if two family members were taken as prisoners of war, they could request to be put together in the same camp. He asked that his brother be transferred to the camp where he was, in Villingen. Władysław was shipped with a truckload of wounded Polish soldiers, who were bound for that same camp. That's how they ended up together in prison camp.

Tadeusz was the prisoner liaison concerning the Geneva Conventions for the prison camp. When Red Cross care packages arrived, Tadeusz signed for them and made sure they were divided equally. Everybody got their parts, and he sent the receipt back to Geneva. To do all that, he was allowed to leave the prison camp and travel to the post office to take care of the business. The guard with him was a soldier who had a heart condition, and so could not go into combat. He was well enough to look after home duties like guarding prisoners. He accompanied him to the post office, and he lived in the same town. So he said he would go home to visit his wife for lunch, and he would meet Tadeusz in the town square at two o'clock in the afternoon. Tadeusz went to the post office to look after his work, and he met the guard exactly at two, as agreed, and they returned to the prison camp together.

Every cigarette was accounted for—my husband was strict. He didn't smoke that much, so he could save his cigarettes and after the war he had enough saved that he was able to buy a BMW sports car with his horde. After the war, cigarettes were worth more than money.

There was an American prisoner who worked in the camp pharmacy. Władysław worked at the hospital, and my husband worked as the interpreter. The three of them lived in the hospital laboratory, though they didn't sleep there. They had a radio also, where they could hear the news from England. They cooked all their food in the laboratory. They were not allowed to have a radio, but the soldiers went to the farmers to work. They traded for a radio, and they built it into the wall. The German guards knew about it (the officers did not), but didn't make any effort to look for it. If it had been the SS running the camp, they would have shot them. But the German regular army guards, they'd ask, "What's new in the war?" They got information this way, and it opened the guards' eyes. The guards were in cahoots with my husband and the other two. They were happy to hear about what was going on in the war.

The pharmacist contrived a way to make alcohol for them, so they had access to 100% alcohol. They had a good time, in a way, because they weren't mistreated. The laboratory was convenient for them. Even their mother was able to send them food packages from Poland.

There was an incident where a prisoner escaped, and was rumored to have found his way back to Poland. The guards found out at roll call, and Tadeusz was questioned, but he said he didn't know anything about it. He was sentenced to two weeks of house arrest. That was the only punishment Tadeusz ever got. They knew that he knew.

Tadeusz got sick and needed to have his tonsils removed, but his brother didn't want to operate on his own family. A German physician came from town to the prison hospital to perform the surgery, and the tonsils came out. Tadeusz didn't have any way of paying him, but he was thankful that the German physician was kind enough to help. Tadeusz visited the family of that physician after the war ended, and as a thank you for having taken his tonsils out in prison camp, he brought them all kinds of good food. At that time, there were things that Germans couldn't get yet, like coffee, tea and chocolate, so in those days it was like getting a million dollars. Villingen was in the occupied French sector, but Tadeusz was able to get American supplies, including chocolate and fruit, which people hadn't seen for a long time. Tadeusz brought him a lot of chocolate, coffee and tea to thank him for the war-time surgery.

They were both in prison there until near the end of the war in 1945, when the Americans eventually liberated Villingen and the camp. The Allied post-war authorities heard about the Kurowskis' facility with languages, they were approached by a French representative of the IRO. The refugees wanted to be with their own people. That's how they got their jobs. With the war over, Germany was flooded with refugees. His brother stayed to work at a hospital in Villingen. Tadeusz lived in Neuenbürg, because it was located in a geographically convenient position for his work—Baden-Baden, and other towns with consulates and embassies were nearby. His chauffeur picked him up every day. From the hospital dining room, I could look straight down the road into the valley, and see the house where he lived.

Tadeusz was in charge of the liaison office for the IRO, arranging all the necessary papers and visas for those seeking to emigrate. They were of every nationality, and included Jewish people, Germans who had run away from the Russians and from Czechoslovakia. They poured into German cities, and houses were temporarily expropriated—the authorities would say to a householder: your house has six rooms, so you would have to move out and six refugee families would move in. They didn't care about your house—you had to move out, and the refugees moved in.

They'd live there until they had all the papers needed to emigrate. Tadeusz would have a list of all the refugees who lived in his region, and in which potential destination countries they had relatives—North America, South America, Africa, anywhere in the world. He would list who needed a passport to South America, or wherever. When he had all the papers together, for perhaps a thousand people, he would organize a train (a regular train, not the cattle truck I arrived in), and they would depart from Karlsruhe, since it had a direct line north to Bremen. The refugees were told they could take only what they could carry. He accompanied them, and put them on the ship. Each person was accounted for, and had all the papers they needed—visa, passport, etc.—and had some money of the country to which they were headed, such as $50. Off they went. When everyone was off the train and on a ship, Tadeusz's mission was over. The ships left, and he went back to start all over again. This might have happened once every four months. He himself emigrated in 1950, so he worked at it for almost five years.

I had seen the same process in Heidenheim, which was not much destroyed since it didn't have much industry. There were many refugees there. It could be a traumatic thing. They were the ones who had survived prisoner of war camps, concentration camps, Germans who had lived in the Sudetenland, in Russia. Katharina the Great had invited German farmers to Russia, long ago. There were German Russians, and after the war they fled back to Germany. There were people like Czechs and Poles who had escaped to the west, to Germany. Germany was largely destroyed, of course, but they ended up in any town that could house them. It was a springboard to emigrate to other countries, and it took five years to get them all placed in other countries. Some of them had relatives, and others just went.

I had a Jewish man, a patient, and he was going to New York. He had a hernia. The country you were going to demanded that you be in good health, so he had to have his hernia fixed. I was working nights at Heidenheim at the time, and I found out from the Mother Superior that he wanted to take me with him; he wanted to marry me! She sternly told him he couldn't do that, but he calmly replied that he would come and steal me in the night. When he was released, maybe two weeks later, he was bound for the United States, and I was careful not to run into him in the street. I was afraid he might kidnap me.

Some of the refugees were sick, and some of them were so ill that they were unable to emigrate. We had a lot of patients with gastro-intestinal problems, whose first nourishment by mouth after the camps had been white wine mixed with an egg and honey. (You have no idea how nutritious the properties of that combination are.) There were no antibiotics. When I was still in Austria, at the hospital in Wels, I heard of penicillin for the first time. But nothing was built up; everything was destroyed, so medicine wasn't yet being manufactured or available in sufficient quantity. If anybody needed antibiotics, you had to send a description of the diagnosis to a panel of American physicians, and they would decide which cases to would be supplied with antibiotics. Afterward, the German pharmaceutical industry started up again, and was able to produce antibiotics.

Russians

I wasn't surprised by the Berlin Blockade of 1948-1949, when the Western allies supplied West Berlin by plane because of the chicanery of the Russians. The refugees told us how the Russians were rude, primitive and cruel.

There was a patient in Stuttgart who was so anemic when she came. She came to die. A woman in Heidenheim had been raped, and was pregnant, though she escaped. The baby was born deformed. She cried. I don't know what eventually happened to the baby.

Władysław's wife, Ursula, said the Russians didn't even know what a flush toilet was. They had wanted to use one to wash potatoes, but when they flushed some of the smaller potatoes were lost. They shot the man who owned the house, because they thought he had sabotaged them.

She told of seeing a boy riding a bicycle in Berlin, without holding his hands on the handlebars. The Russian soldiers thought this was a new invention, and even though they had a bicycle that was better, they traded with him.

One time I met a lady from East Germany at a railroad station. She said, "I hope the train's on time, because I have to be back in the Russian sector by midnight, otherwise I'll be punished." This is how things were under the Russians.

I shared a room in Neuenbürg with another nurse. She came from the eastern part of Germany, and she recounted how she had been raped many times; her mother was raped, too. The Russian soldiers would come with two military trucks, and they cleaned out all the women on a street. One truck would be loaded with all the teenage girls, and the other with their mothers. They would take them away to their camps, and the women would have to work there. They'd clean their barracks, and do their cooking. The women could not lock their doors, and they slept in bunk beds. At night, there'd be drinking, and the soldiers would come and haul the women out of their beds, including the mothers, and then they were raped; gang-raped. There was one girl who, after the third rape one night, bled to death.

One day, one of the Russian officers at that camp just took my nurse friend and married her. The Russian soldiers would go to houses, and just take what they wanted — furniture, clothes, anything they wanted. When they saw your watch, they took it. If you locked your house, they just broke down the door and took everything. He came to her with what he thought would be a wedding gown; it was a nightgown he'd taken from some house. He said, "Put this on, we're getting married." He had a fancy to her. She put it on, and the commandant married them. She didn't like him, of course, but she thought once they're married, the other soldiers ("Thank heaven," she said) would leave her alone. That's what happened. She hated him; she couldn't stand him, but there was a guard with her all time. One night, he got tipsy, and she climbed out through the bathroom window and escaped. She made it out. She was hiding in a barn overnight, and she escaped to the west. She found out her mother was at another Russian camp, and that the same thing had happened to her.

The elderly parents of another woman constructed a bed underneath theirs, so if the Russians came at night, all they saw was an old couple, so nothing happened to their daughter. They also raped old ladies; it didn't matter, when they were drunk.

You could not lock your house against the Russians. If they wanted a sofa, or a chair, they just went into a house and took it — you couldn't do anything about it.

Looking West

Władysław left for Canada in 1950. He chose Peterborough because Canada was advertising for professionals. He could've gone to Montreal, Vancouver, or other cities, but for some reason he liked Peterborough. He actually had a professorship in Berlin in obstetrics and gynecology offered, because he was fluent in German, but he turned them down. He had to do his internship again to earn a Canadian medical license. He then did a repeat fellowship in obstetrics and gynecology.

He was a longtime smoker, and developed Buerger's disease. His leg was always blue, because the veins did not properly recirculate the blood. He had his leg amputated below the knee, in approximately 1954. He decided to leave Canada after that, because he found it hard to stand on his prosthesis when it was cold and damp. If the stump became wet, there was breakdown of tissue. He looked for a country that was consistently warm, and ended up studying psychiatry so he could work at a military hospital in Arizona. He worked there until he was in his late sixties — they did not want to let him go. They had one daughter, and he worked long so they could put her through university. They enjoyed their retirement; they had a house in Mexico near a beach. He died of cancer in 1986 or 1987.

I knew that the hospital in Neuenbürg was paying relatively poorly for 12 hours of work each day. Tadeusz knew about his, too. He suggested I go to Switzerland, where the pay was better, and they were looking for nurses. The expectation was I would follow the Kurowskis to Canada later — he said, "You have to come to us."

I had to ask the director of the hospital in Neuenbürg for permission to leave. They let me go, but with regret. I was quietly gratified that my dedication and hard work had been recognized; a physician wrote in a letter of reference (in German), "never-tired, wonderful care; one of the most-loved nurses; always willing and kind; good sense of humor; our hospital will lose one of our best nurses."

Tadeusz was himself highly respected as an efficient, trustworthy and responsible person — when I was preparing to leave the country, I didn't even have to apply for a visa to Switzerland; his word to the authorities was good enough. He knew every embassy of every state. We went to the consulate, and he vouched for me — she is of good character —

and that was how I was able to get a visa. You normally never got such a thing without a formal application in writing.

1951 Burgdorf, Switzerland

I moved to Burgdorf, Switzerland in April of 1951. Tadeusz told me that his wife had cancer, and that her future was bad. He never promised marriage, but in my heart I knew this was the one I wanted to spend the rest of my life with. But he never made any promises whatsoever. He took me to the train station for my move to Switzerland, and I almost got off the train—it was so painful to separate from him. He left shortly after, still in April, to emigrate to Canada.

Although I had changed countries, with the compactness of Europe I had moved only about 250 kilometers. Burgdorf was lovely. The residence I lived in was near Bern, the city center of which is only about 20 kilometers from the hospital, which was a district hospital. It had balconies, and you could see mountains, the Bernese Alps. Our residence was beautiful—modern, almost like a hotel—with flowers and shrubs outside, and inside a common room with television, radio and a library. You worked from six o'clock in the morning until eight in the evening, but there were two hours of rest allotted over noontime. Usually after lunch, everybody would sleep—we were tired.

We got a half-day off each week, either morning or afternoon, and another day off once a month. Whoever was off would bicycle with friends, visiting perhaps the parents of another nurse who lived in the mountains nearby. It would be about two hours, uphill, downhill; we'd stay overnight, though we'd have to get up at five to be on duty at the hospital in time. Otherwise, we might go up into the mountains some more. There would a restaurant or a cafeteria; you could always eat somewhere up there. Typically, we would get some farmer's bread, and a big chocolate bar. Up in the mountains, there were cows and there were cafeterias, and you could get fresh cow's milk. This was our lunch. We'd go home again after sightseeing. In winter, there was always a ski hill close by. There wasn't much time with our work schedule, but I was able to ski a little bit. Working long hours, and having only Sunday morning or Sunday afternoon off, you were so tired. I didn't have much time to spend on skiing, but you could always tell by the commotion if someone had fallen and broken a leg or something like that, and ended up at the hospital.

In Switzerland, you could sunbathe in March, although there were sometimes strong winds. We had a protected place in the garden, with an awning, surrounded by flowers.

I often worked nights, relieving the head nurse on a different floor each shift. I might work one day in the nursery, the next day on the medical floor, and the next day after that on the surgical floor. The night shift meant eight o'clock in the evening until eight o'clock in the morning—twelve hours.

The Burgdorf hospital was Protestant, which still meant Lutheran. I went to the church service they had, but if I had a Sunday morning off, I sometimes went to the Catholic church. I was always impressed with the Catholic mass. There was something missing from the Protestant service, but I didn't know what it was. Somehow it wasn't as fulfilling for my spiritual needs.

I was always in contact with one church or another. Sunday just wasn't right for me if I wasn't in a church, for some reason. I was accustomed from my childhood home to going to church every Sunday, where my father played the organ. Church was a part of your life. The spiritual atmosphere is sort of ingrained into you. There was respect for my father, but there was something about going to church. At that time, I probably didn't recognize that I was inspired by the Holy Spirit.

I took art at school, and we visited churches to study the architecture. We had to put something on our heads, as a sign of respect; otherwise we wouldn't have been allowed to go in. I didn't go to church at that time (during the war) — I was completely empty. I didn't go to church for faith, only for architecture! My faith was nourished, it wasn't mentioned, it wasn't practiced; it had been put to sleep. This came out after, when I was in the Catholic hospital in Austria. It came all alive when I saw the soldiers going to church, and I wondered how that could be. That's where the seed started to grow.

* * *

The pay was much better; maybe triple what I had been getting in Neuenbürg. I put my money in the bank, because I knew that I would be going to Canada, sooner or later. The one thing I knew about Canada was Niagara Falls, and I had always wished that I could see it. I had no idea what the weather was like. Tadeusz and I exchanged letters every two weeks or so, and his included descriptions of the countryside around Peterborough for me.

The year 1951 was a time when Canada was still advertising for professionals to come. There were advertisements in the newspapers and on the radio. Canada had about 14 million people then, and they said they needed professionals. A lot of people went because they had struggled after the war, many having lost their houses, and they thought it was an opportunity to build another new life. There were political emigrants, but I was more of a 'compassionate' emigrant. I wasn't a domestic emigrant. Some had sponsors, allowing them to work for years as a maid or similar. I paid for my own ticket, but many had their trips paid for by their future employer, and they had to work there to pay off the money.

I applied to emigrate. I went to the consulate in Karlsruhe, Germany, and applied for Canada. (The Kurowskis had gone to Canada; if they had gone to the United States, I would have gone to the United States. My brother-in-law interned in Peterborough; that's why I went there.) You had to have proof that you had no criminal record, that you didn't owe any income tax, that you had never been in trouble. Then, you would get your visa from the Canadian government. You had to have a health report, and give a urine specimen. I had to have all my teeth checked, but there were no problems of any kind. I have always been healthy.

It was made easier that Tadeusz and his brother were already there, and were waiting for me. It was like I had a family to go to. I wasn't going into a completely unknown situation; I had some support. Other people had no support at all. I had no parents any more. My hardest decision was to leave my little sister, but there were so many competing reasons — some to stay, some to go. For the latter: I wanted a new life; I hoped to get married; I loved to travel; it was a new and exciting country; I knew I had friends waiting for me. But I knew I would have to leave my heritage behind me. It wasn't easy; it was a bittersweet farewell.

I stayed in Switzerland until November, 1952. I left Burgdorf for the last time on November 26th. I stayed with my brother Hans in Crailsheim in Germany for two or three weeks before I left for Canada by ship.

When I left, Europe was a mess, but was building up. Germany still had a lot of damage from all the bombing in the war. Where my brother lived, in Crailsheim, it was practically 90% destroyed. There was constantly building going on. That's why they asked for so many people to come from Turkey and Morocco to help rebuild. The original thinking was that when the foreign workers were finished, they'd go back home, though it didn't work out that way.

It was a hard decision, regarding what to take and what to leave. I packed everything that would fit, and left behind what I couldn't take with me. I took some of my books and clothes, and some mementoes and souvenirs that meant something to me. You could take only so much. I had too big wooden boxes made, by a carpenter. They were about the size of a regular dresser; not too big. I had my suitcases, one the old Pullman kind with layers. I still have it, now down in my garage with old Christmas decorations in it. This is what I packed my belongings in. There were clothes my brother and sister-in-law gave me. Even some dishes I wanted—an assortment of things. On top of each item, inside, I put some nursing item, such as a nursing degree, or a nursing cap. When I arrived in Canada, I believe this is why they never even bothered to look through my luggage—everyone else had to unpack all their luggage (what a mess!). I don't even know what they were looking for. But when they saw I was a nurse, they were satisfied that there was no need to search. My brother said not to worry about over-filling the suitcase, as he would close it for me.

I didn't have much money. Before I left, I was in contact with the banker I dealt with in Switzerland, and I asked him for the best exchange rate between the new German and Swiss currencies. He kept an eye on it for me, and he told me one day that the exchange rates were good. I exchanged the money for German currency, and kept it for my departure. After I had paid for the trip, I was carried what was left over with me (about 200 Canadian dollars), and I kept it in a place that I was sure they wouldn't look if they searched me.

I traveled to the port at Bremen, in northern Germany, sending my two big boxes in the freight part of the train. This train was specifically designated for emigrants. We had food given to us on the trip. When I arrived at Bremen, we were put in a barracks overnight—not a hotel, but a place where refugees stayed. I opened my suitcase, and there was a letter on top, from my brother. He said how sorry he was I was leaving, but that he knew I had to look after my future. He assured me that if anything went wrong in Canada, "…please, please, come back; we love you." You don't have to suffer, he said; come back if you need to. I cried when I read the letter.

We boarded the ship, a Greek liner named *Neptunia*. There were probably at least 300 passengers. It seemed like everyone had someone to wave goodbye to them, but I didn't. There was a band playing a song that was popular at the time: *"Auf Wiedersehen, auf Wiedersehen,"* they sang. I was pretty strong, until the man next to me cried, and then I cried. (I can easily cry!) Up until then I'd been really strong. I didn't have anybody to see me off, no relatives there, because no one I knew could travel to Bremen.

It was probably a combination of being German—you always had to be strong—and also it was my own temperament, because I knew I was then on strange waters (literally), and that I shouldn't waver on it. If I had wavered, it would have been even worse. I had made up my mind to go, so there was no sense to dwell on it, after the fact, about whether I should or should not be going. I had made the decision, and I was standing by it. I would not go back and forth, back and forth. After we left the port—that was that.

There were moments before in my life when I had to be strong, and I knew I had to get on with it.

I knew that I would be married eventually. If Tadeusz's first wife had outlived me, it would have been another drastic disappointment. But he and I were good friends, regardless, and I knew I could rely on him, and on his brother. They gave me courage to start over. All my life after I lost my parents, God rewarded me with good people. Good people with good principles that I could look up to. People that were smarter than me. People that were kind. These were the kinds of people I met all along, and so I didn't have to always ask, "Why did I lose my parents?" I couldn't use that as an excuse, because God knew what he was doing. I was rewarded one-hundredfold (and more) with meeting good people.

On board the ship, I hadn't had the choice of my class of ticket. It was configured for refugee transport, and everybody got the same food and the same accommodations. My cabin had bunk beds, with three other people sharing the room.

I was seasick for the twelve days it took to cross the Atlantic Ocean. A lot of people were sick. I had my first and last meal, that first evening. Afterward I went up on deck; I turned to someone and said, "Do you feel funny?" She said, "Yes." In response, I vomited into the ocean. I thought I was going to die. Even water I would bring up. I was really, really sick. Eventually, I couldn't have cared less whether I lived or died.

I spent a lot of my time sleeping on deck, because in the winter time the Gulf Stream warmed up the air, and it was better out there. I talked a bit with a lady who was traveling with her daughter. They were bound for Hamilton, Ontario, where she had a job waiting for her.

Mostly, I didn't feel like having a conversation.

7. Becoming Canadian

1952 Peterborough, Canada

My New Country

Neptunia and I arrived at the port of Halifax, on Canada's east coast, on December 22, 1952.

It was in winter, near Christmastime. When I saw the rocks of the shore, I was surprised at how barren it all looked. I thought, "Oh, my goodness, if this is Canada, I may have made a mistake." Where I came from, there were no bare rocks, but vineyards and forests. In Europe, you might see rocks by the shore or up in the mountains, but there were always trees. I felt all of a sudden homesick, and despite my vow, I wondered about whether I had made the right decision.

There was a nice steward on the ship who said to me as we neared port, "You haven't eaten anything the whole trip, so I'll go make you some sandwiches that you can take with you." When I went through customs at Pier 21, they didn't look through my suitcases, but they did take my sandwiches away. "You can't take food from the ship onto land," they said to me.

There was such a rush in getting off the ship, and looking around and finding everything. Everyone was checked out and unpacking and packing. You didn't have much time to observe anything; it was just a matter of getting out of there, and getting to the train or whatever the next step was.

The Kurowski brothers and Władysław's wife had sent me instructions on what to do and where to go. They had a train ticket and some Canadian money waiting for me, and I had to go to the Halifax railway station to pick it up. I went to a cafeteria, though these were not known in Europe then. Someone told me I could go there and choose what food I wanted, so I thought I'd try it out. When I got there, I saw a house cat sitting on top of one of the tables. I read the menu, and I didn't know what 'hog dog' meant, but I knew what 'dog' meant. Hot dog. I knew there was no way that I was willing to eat a dog. I left, knowing that a place with a cat on the table and a dog on the menu was no place for me. I got some crackers somewhere.

I went to the telephone to tell my friends in Peterborough I had arrived, and to thank them for the ticket. As I walked around, I was surprised to hear my name being called. I had forgotten my train ticket in the telephone booth, and some kind person had found it and turned it in.

The first leg of the train trip would be to the city of Montreal, in the province of Quebec, a distance of about 1,200 kilometers, which would take about 20 hours. The second leg would be from Montréal, Québec, to Port Hope, Ontario, about 450 kilometers and six hours. From there would be a car ride of about 50 kilometers, 45 minutes, to my final destination, Peterborough, Ontario. (This trip covers about one-quarter of the 'width' of Canada. Traveling 1,700 kilometers by train in Europe, by comparison, would have gotten me from Edinburgh in Scotland to Madrid, Spain, including a ferry trip across the English Channel.)

We were all put on the oldest train in Canada. The overhead compartment where you put your luggage was large enough that you could have slept in there. The windows didn't open, and it was so hot that even the cold water in the washrooms was hot. The trains in Europe were much different—you could at least open the window!

When I looked out as we were travelling, all I could see was snow and flat, flat, flat countryside. I tried to sleep as we travelled, but it was too hot. I was still weak from not eating much on the ship.

When I arrived in Montréal we had about an hour to wait for the connecting train, on the way to Port Hope in Ontario.

I got out of the train in Montréal, but I didn't know that we had to switch to a train on another track. I followed my curiosity, and walked about a bit to see what it all looked like. We had learned a little bit about the city (and Niagara Falls!) in geography. I finished my looking around until it was time to go. I returned to my train, but my train wasn't there. Oh, my goodness! I panicked. I asked an official, and fortunately I could speak enough to make my problem understood. I was so upset, that what came out was a mixture of rudimentary schoolgirl French and mashed English: refugee…Halifax…train…Port Hope. He pieced together what I wanted, and took me three tracks further over, and I was able to get on the right train.

I arrived in Port Hope at six o'clock in the morning on December 24, 1952. It had been two days since we had set out from Halifax.

Tadeusz had said he and his brother would be at the station there to meet me in a Morris Minor car. It had been two years since I had last seen Tadeusz, and three years since I had seen Władysław.

Everywhere I looked it was snow and flat. The station in Port Hope was like a tiny house; I was used to stations in Europe that were 'real,' substantial railroad stations, but this looked like a little workshop. No one was there. No Tadeusz, no Władysław. There I stood with my thin suitcases (the trunks had been sent separately to Peterborough by another train) in the early cold winter morning. Six o'clock in the morning, and lots of snow, but no souls other than me. Another mistake I'd made!

The station master came along, and he opened the little house and put a wood fire on. We exchanged just a few words, but there was still no sign of the Kurowskis.

It turned out there were two railroad stations in Port Hope—one for the Canadian Pacific line, and a completely separate one for the Canadian National line. My friends had gone to the wrong one. Having waited for a while there, they eventually asked where the train from Montréal was. They found out how things worked, figured out they were at the wrong station, and finally arrived at the one where I was.

We drove up Highway 28 to Peterborough, and it was picturesque. It had been awful, arriving with nobody around, but things were better now. I was happy.

It was right before Christmas, and Władysław's wife had everything ready for me. They had rented a room for me in a nearby house, and there were flowers and fruit waiting for me in it when I arrived there for the first time. I had a room upstairs with a small kitchen, in a family home on Stewart Street.

I spent Christmas with the Kurowskis, and we went to church together. Tadeusz had a rented room with some Polish people on Rogers Street, and Władysław was just off Reid Street. Władysław was an intern by then, but he had to sleep at the hospital except for his one day off a week. After he finished, they moved to a house where their daughter was born.

Tadeusz tried to learn enough English to get back into agriculture again, but the government said that he would have to re-train at a Canadian university to be qualified for a Canadian license. He inquired about work with the University of Guelph, thinking he might be able to work in a laboratory there, given his experience. He would have had to have been a Canadian citizen, however, which required a five-year waiting period.

Regardless, they deemed him to be over-qualified. He turned to private tutoring in Russian and French, working with students and adults in Peterborough. He asked the director of the local school board about the possibility of his teaching high school Russian or French. They said, of course, that he'd have to take university courses to qualify. He didn't have the money—he'd lost all his money, too, during the war. He kept on with the private tutoring. He eventually took an accounting course, and he worked as a credit union accountant at the Peterborough Civic Hospital.

He showed me Immaculate Conception church in the east part of the city, where he went. I had moved to a room on Reid Street, upstairs from a printing business. When I looked out my new window, I could see St. Peter's Cathedral, which wasn't far away. I walked over to St. Peter's for mass, but I couldn't find anyone I knew. It turned out the Kurowskis were going to Immaculate Conception, and I was at the wrong one.

Władysław's wife, Ursula, was a pediatric nurse at the hospital, and she negotiated a position there on my behalf. I knew that I would be able to start in February at the Civic Hospital in town, but after Christmas, she found a one-month contract for me. It was with a local private nursing home, on Monaghan Road (it's now the parking lot of General Electric). She knew the director, and she said if I worked there first, maybe I could get used to the medical terms in English, and nursing practice in Canada, before I started at a hospital. I worked there for a month, but when I went to the bank to cash my first paycheck, it bounced. Another bad experience. Władysław's wife took charge and said that was finished, that I wasn't going there again. I'd be starting at the hospital soon, anyway.

Nursing Assistant Once More

At the hospital, I would have to work for a year as a nursing assistant rather than a nurse. This would be until I could speak English well enough, and all my certification papers had been verified through the Canadian and German nursing associations. I had all my papers translated into English—they told me everything I needed, the Canadian Nurses Association in Toronto.

I had good reference letters from physicians and groups with whom I had worked. This was one of the letters to the Canadian Nurses Association, from the *Deutsches Rotes Kreuz*: "Brigitte has worked with the German Red Cross as an assistant nurse during the years 1944-45. She has joined a nursing school recognized by the state of Karl-Olga Hospital in Stuttgart. She passed her examination in general nursing on September 30, 1947 with good results." I had 500 hours of practical training there. From the *Krankenhaus* in Neuenbürg: "Enthusiastic, happy, well-liked by patients and personnel, friendly, pleasant personality, happy attitude loved by everybody."

I started my new job in February, 1953 with four different dictionaries, and I carried a little dictionary with me in my pocket all the time: *One Thousand Words in English*. I couldn't speak much English when I first came to Canada. I had to work right away, and so couldn't go to night school for English because I had to work shifts. Can you imagine trying to work with patient charts in a different language? I had my little dictionary in my pocket, and when I had something to ask, I checked it for the pronunciation. A constant challenge was emphasis: in German, for example, the emphasis is on the first syllable of 'thermometer.' The word's spelled the same in English, but the emphasis is on the second syllable. Well, I had trouble with this. The first time I went in and said, "Good morning, good morning! I'm going to take your temperature—here's the thermometer." They laughed, of course, since I had used the German pronunciation for 'thermometer.' After that, if I wasn't quite sure about a new word or term, I'd make sure to look first in my little book, and then I 'busted it out.'

My first patients were men who had suffered strokes. Before I went in a patient's room, I would practice pronouncing words, like 'thermometer.' At first, I had trouble phonetically distinguishing some English sounds, such as between 'pen' and 'pan.' Patients would ask for me for a pan (a bedpan) and I would bring a pen. They got a kick out of it.

The patients teased me sometimes. One time a man asked for a cola soft drink, but I knew he was a heart patient and couldn't have it. I told him I'd go see if he could have any. "What's your name," I asked. "Murphy," he said. I went to the desk, told them that Mr. Murphy wanted something, and they laughed and laughed. I asked them why. They said he was teasing me, and that his name wasn't Murphy. Apparently, that was an old joke, with 'visiting Mrs. Murphy' meaning using the toilet. (Even today, I still don't understand why that was funny.)

Before I left Europe, I had taken a six-week course in the basics of English—phrasing and a few words. I mostly learned on the job in Canada. I read newspapers, and had the Kurowskis and other people talk to me in English to help me learn. It was a year before I could read and write English well enough to go to nursing school.

I still have my little book, *One Thousand Words in English*.

***

My grandmother died in 1953, and was buried in the family grave in Ilshofen. I did not attend her funeral, mainly for pecuniary reasons, but there was not much love between us. Maybe I did not understand her, but I pray to this day for her departed soul.

She remembered me in her will, with the money from the sale of her house in Ilshofen divided among we three surviving children (Hans, Liselotte and me). I left my part with my little sister, because she was paying for her own house at the time.

Back to School

Some people told me that it was unfair that I had to do my education all over again, but I accepted this. It was a new country, with new customs. If you don't want to do it, you can leave. I worked with a former German physician at Sick Children's hospital, who was then working as a nursing assistant. She said she was too old to go to school again, but she couldn't get work as either a doctor or a nurse. You couldn't break the rules; that was just the way it was.

I thought this was only right, I didn't think it was wrong to be up to the same standard as other Canadian professionals. I was quite pleased to do that, and I enjoyed it. I had to start all over again, but it gave me a new life, a new outlook. I wanted to make something of myself, and to go back and get my degree again. I wanted to contribute to Canada—they were good to me.

The Civic hospital building was fairly new when I came to Peterborough; just two years old, with 240 beds. The nursing school was in a dedicated building adjacent to the hospital, and included laboratories. After the bombed-out places I was used to, I was impressed with the Civic. It was a different style, and set-up. I put my whole heart and soul into it, and I was determined to succeed. I knew I'd have to do my degree again, and I concentrated on that. So did the Kurowskis. While I was studying and living in residence, they brought me food every day because I wasn't getting paid.

There were no tuition fees, though I did pay for the books (the hospital loaned me money for this, which I paid back after I graduated). There was no salary. Tadeusz and Władysław helped me with money.

I entered the school of nursing in September 1954. They didn't accept the year that was accredited to me in Germany, so they said you only have two years, so you have to do the whole nursing training, everything, again. I started out with everything, being in school and the lectures and everything else. I only needed less time for the practical work. Where normally it would take three months to learn things on a surgical floor, I might take two weeks or something like that. I crammed wherever I could, and I did the whole three years in fifteen months. I started every morning at four o'clock.

We were taught by nursing instructors and physicians. During one lecture early on, we were discussing the vital organs, and the brain. I didn't know what they meant by 'vital.' Usually, I left blanks for words I didn't understand, and at the end of the class, I would borrow someone else's notes so I could put the words in where the blanks were. Instead of *vy'-tle*, we said *vee-tal'* in German, so once I figured that out I had to go back and fill in the spaces I'd left. Sometimes I'd miss my lunch hour filling in the blanks.

Discussing surgery another time, I heard of an 'acute' case, and all I could think about was 'cute.' What could be so cute about an appendix? When you learn a language, you don't always hear all the sounds, or readily grasp all the minutiae.

At the end of each lecture came a question period, and I asked most of the questions. This kept the other students longer, so sometimes they reminded me not to ask too many.

One time I was really depressed, and I went to the hospital through the tunnel that connected it with the nurses' residence. There was a doctor there, and he was kind funny in the way he dealt with people—he either liked you or not. I didn't know then what he even saw in me as a student. He stopped me, and asked me how I was doing. I was so surprised that he spoke to me. I told him I wondered if I could make it, as I was really low that day. My proud instructor didn't allow me to be downcast. He said, "Listen, kiddo, you'll make out all right." It gave me such a lift, and helped me to make it through the day. I really needed that lift.

When I was in nursing school, I worked weekends on the floor—I had to get familiar with the practical parts. On the weekends, I was mostly in the diet kitchen, preparing things like diabetic foods or formula for the nursery. I didn't mind, because the other students had to write case studies about their patients.

The nursing examinations I had in Europe were all given orally, delivered by the physicians who taught us. In Canada, they were all written. Tadeusz and Władysław were supportive in everything, and they were eager for me to do well. We wrote exams in every subject.

I first wrote the first-year exams at the Civic, and after the first examination, the instructor called me into her office and asked me to answer all the questions orally that I had written on the exam paper. I had written all my answers in English, but with German grammar, so she couldn't understand what I had written. I passed, but it was my first exam trial. After that, I wrote the second-year, and finally the third-year exams. I passed all the exams, and graduated in 1956 from the nursing school at Civic Hospital with the third-year students. I then wrote the registration exams in Toronto for accreditation as a registered nurse, and I passed everything. In the spring of 1956, I was officially designated as a Canadian RN. I was the first non-Canadian who graduated from Peterborough.

After the graduation ceremony in August, I went to a pediatric hospital in Toronto, The Hospital for Sick Children, for a further compulsory three months. At Sick Kids, I worked with gastrointestinal disease patients for a month; they had me practically in charge there. I lived at a residence near the hospital, and there were all kinds of nursing students from all over Ontario there. You could tell by the uniform the hospital each student had come from.

We were really proud of our uniforms. I worked for a month with hydrocephalic patients—oh, but they were temperamental. I worked for a month on the medical floor, with babies. There was an Eskimo baby, and I always ended up feeding her last. She was so content, where the others were screaming. She didn't like the food, and we didn't know what she was used to eating, so I said we need some whale blubber! She was about two years old. To get her to eat, I had to squeeze her nose to encourage her to open her mouth to breathe, and then I quickly put the food in her mouth.

When I was at Sick Kids, I was so inspired by the medicine, by the environment, if I had the money I would have gone to university. But I didn't have the money. I came practically penniless to Peterborough. So did my first husband, from Poland, they lost everything to the Russians. Life would have been different. I never asked, "Why did my parents die? Why this? Why me?" and yet I missed them awfully. Even when I saw a mother just straightening out a girl's skirt, this made me jealous. No, not jealous, really; not envious. But it hurt. I never asked, "Why?" I never was bitter.

Full-fledged Nurse

After I graduated, I put in my application for full-time work immediately.

I had wonderful letters of reference from Sick Children's in Toronto, and they had even asked me to come back to work there. However, I chose to work for the Peterborough Civic Hospital. It wasn't just that the Peterborough hospital had offered me a job, but also that I felt a loyalty to them because they were good to me, too, and I had told them that I would work there.

I worked on the surgical floor for about three or four months, and then there came an opening in the operating room, and I worked there from then until I retired in August, 1989.

I was still a German citizen. When I went into training, in order to graduate I had to agree to become a Canadian citizen, and abandon my German citizenship. We had to learn the oath, and I was concerned about saying all the words correctly. It was a big challenge, and a big change. I was almost overwhelmed at how far I had come, and that I would finally be initiated as a Canadian.

I became a Canadian citizen in Peterborough, having fulfilled the required waiting period of five years, in June, 1958. There was an article in the local newspaper, *The Peterborough Examiner*, about me. I still have the clipping; they described me as an "olive-skinned native of Germany," the first non-Canadian to graduate from the Civic Hospital school of nursing, and that I had done the whole three years in fifteen months.

Being a German in one of the Allied countries, with a heavy German accent, I wasn't mistreated anywhere, or discriminated against, except for two occasions. One was a nurse who said I was German, and we had started the war, and therefore we had "no right to be here" (in Canada). The other was a patient, just after I had returned to Peterborough after finishing my pediatric training in Toronto. I was in a wonderful mood, feeling really, really good. The next morning, I was assigned to a medical floor at the Peterborough hospital. The first patients I visited were two ladies in one room. It was cold outside that day. The lady by the window had it open. When I went in, I said good morning, and the lady by the door said, "Oh, I am so cold. The lady in the next bed, she wants the window open." I said, "We'll get you a bath now, and I'll close the window." After I closed the window, I turned around and approached this lady, who was next to the window. She sat up in her bed, slapped me in the face, and said, "You get out of this country. You started the war. You lost the war."

Those things happened, and you had to carry them with you.

I didn't say anything. I went out of the room, reported it to the supervisor, and said I was not going back to that room, and there was nothing they could say to make me go back to that room. I had always been told that the patient was always right, so if this was their policy, then I can't do anything about it. It didn't mean it was right. It was a lady who had a pet shop in town. She promised that when she died, all her property would be sold, and the proceeds would go to the hospital. When they told me the patient was always right, and didn't do anything about it, I assume they did it because of the money. (It turned out, when she died, that she didn't have any money.)

The doctors teased me sometimes, saying things like, "No wonder Germany lost the war!" I would reply, "Not because of me. I did my best!"

When the doctors were talking together outside the operating room, and I'd go out to tell them we were ready for them, they would sometimes dawdle. I'd say, "On the double! It's the German Army calling!" They put up with me.

It went both ways, though. Later, one of the staff physicians had a beard, and looked a little like the actor Burt Reynolds. I'd open the door and say, "I'm looking for Burt Reynolds!" How he'd leap up to come out!

Adjusting From Europe to North America

Canada was different. The buildings were different—at first I thought Peterborough was an ugly town. You don't see any telephone wires up above ground in Europe. All the telephone wires in North America made it such a messy look. The houses were not the same. The architecture was not the same. I wasn't used to it. It was a real shock to me. I must say, I wasn't impressed with Peterborough, the whole appearance of the town.

At first, I didn't know the people, but I got to know them fast, at the hospital and elsewhere. There were some who were distant; there were some who were despising me for being German. Most of the time, I didn't have bad experiences—I was slapped in the face by only one patient. The food was different than German food, but I was hooked on ice cream for a while (until I stopped it, when I saw that I had gained weight). There was ice milk in Europe then, but it was more like sherbet. The food was good, and it was a new experience. I never complained about food, because we had been without for so long.

I was still smoking; I had smoked for 11 years. I started as a joke in boarding school, to see if we'd get caught. It wasn't real smoking, because we didn't have money to buy cigarettes. We did once in a while, but we weren't hooked on it. After the war, especially when I was at Neuenbürg, in the French zone, I smoked early in the morning. I'd wake up with a hungry stomach, and smoking would take the hunger feeling away. So, I smoked. Władysław was responsible for me getting off the cigarettes, because he lost his leg due to cigarettes and Buerger's disease. I ended up with esophagitis, and Władysław said smoking had an effect like acid, and that the best thing was for us all to quit together. "You help yourselves," he said to Tadeusz and me, "and I'll help myself." That's what we did, all together, in 1954.

I was so lucky to have met Tadeusz and his brother. It could not have been just a coincidence. I clung to this. This was my goal. I would stick with these people. They were a good influence on me, and I felt happy. This really was a healing process, having left Europe behind. They were Europeans, too, so there was a continuity of tradition and lifestyle.

I can remember the old post office on the corner of Hunter and Water Streets in Peterborough—it isn't there anymore, demolished in the mid-1950s. It was an old building, in the European style, and I went there many times, because I was homesick for Europe. Just looking at the building gave me almost an osmosis for absorbing European atmosphere. It looked somehow more organized and orderly, and reminded me of Europe.

I missed the whole atmosphere of Europe. There is a German word for the feeling; it's called *Gemütlichkeit*. You can't describe it; it has no translation—the whole atmosphere, the ambience. You didn't have to belong to a club there to have some fun or some entertainment. Everything was easily available. You would have those coffee houses. You'd meet people. When you went to a restaurant, you wouldn't just sit by yourself; they'd put you with some other people. Or you'd ask people at a table, "Would you allow me to sit with you here?" and they'd say, "Sure." You were always with people there, you were never alone. When I'm at a restaurant in Canada, I'm always seated by myself. Even if there was a person sitting at a table with two seats, it wouldn't be customary here to ask, "May I sit with you?" They'd think I'm 'funny.' Over there, it was acceptable. If, for example, you went for an evening out to a famous wine pub, and there was music playing, people would get up and dance. It didn't even have to be staged—if you felt like dancing, then you danced, and it was acceptable. You could go and get a glass of beer, and sit in your front garden and have it there. You didn't have to go to a liquor store, or get a license. Everyone was free about it, but for the most part it wasn't abused, either. Restaurants wouldn't serve someone who was drunk, because the owner of the restaurant would lose their reputation. So many things were just different.

The atmosphere there was homey. On a Sunday afternoon, if you went for a walk in a park or a village, there would be a band playing. You'd walk around, all very nice, and you'd have coffee, and you'd meet people. Now, they have outdoor coffee available here, modeling Europe. But transposing that atmosphere here is not the same; you can't have the same atmosphere here as you could over there.

Europe today is still like that in the smaller places. It has changed with the American influence over there—it's been 'American-ized.' It still is like this. I think the children there are still a little more disciplined. They may not think so, but I do. Discipline. You were taught that you stand when an older person comes into the room; you don't sit. If somebody drops something, you pick it up for them. You open doors for people. In my days there, you said to anybody you met, "*Grüß Gott.*" '*Grüß*' is a greeting, and '*Gott*' is God. Whenever you saw anybody, whether you knew them or not, you'd say, "*Grüß Gott.*" It was entirely different.

The attitude was being freer in things. After the war started, I noticed a bigger freedom for everything. One time in Peterborough I was waiting for a bus to go to the hospital, and a patient drove by in a Cadillac. He was wearing sloppy clothes. In Europe, if you drove an expensive car, you dressed accordingly. Everything fit together. I was talking to a patient one time who was displeased with his physician, and he said, "Who does that doctor think he is? Just because he's a doctor. He has a car, I have a car. He has a refrigerator, I have a refrigerator. He has a TV, I have one." I wondered that he seemed to base his judgment of someone on their material things. In Europe, everything fit together. Here, there's opportunity to get easier things. Like credit cards; it took me a long time to get used to using credit cards to buy things. People thought they could buy culture with money. Canada, to me, developed technology fast, but the people didn't change as fast with it. Naturally, I'm integrated now, and used to it. Still, when I go to Europe now and I see with different eyes, I can see people there take things for granted. Just like here, some people who live in Peterborough have never gone over the lift lock—they take it for granted. It's human nature.

I had to buy some detergent one time to wash my clothes, but I didn't know the name for it. I had to ask somebody where to get the powder for washing, and they told me about the A&P grocery store on Aylmer Street. When I got there, I went in the wrong door, and it was a bar, for men only (it was right beside the grocery store). There they were, smoking and drinking beer. I was completely lost, and they all looked at me. I finally found the right door.

When I was ready to pay for the groceries, I found that someone had stolen my wallet. I had a cloth shopping bag (in Europe, people always carried their own bags with them, often nicely done) with my wallet in it, but when I got to the cashier it was gone. It was my first week in Peterborough. I also had in my wallet pictures of my family: my mother, my father, us when we were young. All those I lost too. Otherwise I would have more of my brothers and so on. I was so embarrassed, and I didn't speak enough English to explain. Nevertheless, the cashier understood. I had to leave the food there, and I had to back and ask Władysław's wife for money, after which I was able to go back and get the food.

I missed the church bells terribly. In Germany, every church's bells rang every Sunday, and it did not seem like Sunday without them. They had such an emotional meaning. You'd hear many bells together, not just one. Every town and village has various bells that you'll here before church begins.

I liked the food in Canada. I didn't mind it whatsoever. However, the first time I tried a cola soft drink, my hands started to shake because of the caffeine. That was my first and last cola.

Some vegetables were new to me. I had never eaten the green part of the celery. In Germany, it was grown for the root, and the root was cooked and eaten. The stalks were not considered edible.

Christmas is celebrated on Christmas Eve in Germany, and the stores close at three o'clock. In Canada, the stores were open late, to six or seven.

People could afford cars and big electric appliances, regardless of their salary. Germany had it too, but I always lived in hospitals. It was new to see people all with their own houses, and with cottages. It's wonderful with all the lakes, because Germany doesn't many lakes. I never felt safe in winter, with the slippery snow and ice, and I had to get used to it.

Over there, the main meal is at lunch, and the evening is just a light meal. At four o'clock you pause from work, and have coffee and cake, perhaps even at a coffee house. In summertime, people go and have a cup of coffee in a little cup, with a little pitcher of milk and a little sugar bowl. If you want another cup, you have to buy it—there are no refills. Everything's served on a little doily. It's like a little afternoon ceremony, and especially so on Sunday afternoons. There were no sweet desserts after meals in Germany, but now, I like dessert. In Rome, do what the Romans do. I easily got used to the Canadian style.

In most of the cities there's a bandstand in the park, and after church you promenade to the bandstand. A band plays, and there's music, which I missed when I came to Canada.

In Europe the churches were all architecture—from the Gothic and Renaissance times. The cathedrals were all old-style. In Peterborough, they were different. St. Peter's Cathedral reminded me a little more of the European style, than the newer ones. I always felt a little more at home at St. Peter's. It wasn't that they weren't nice, just that I was more used to the old-fashioned ones with the architecture and art. We had the attitude that it was a new country, a young country. Therefore, accept it. It's wasn't that you didn't see the difference, or that it was "I wish I was back there," as some people said. Instead, I had made up my mind to come here, and so I was going to accept. I'm used to it now. People change. Times change. You have to go through the process of a new environment, and accept it. Not everything over in Europe is nice, either!

This is home for me, now. There are people who invite me to their homes. It's also a funny thing sometimes, that people who you thought you could count on desert you. It happened to me after my first husband died; couples who had always invited us over, afterward I never heard a word from them. I've made my own friends, and some friends accepted me, which is good and wonderful. I feel so good among families, because I didn't have the family atmosphere for a long time. I had fun with my brothers; this is what a family should be.

The capacity and knowledge of the medical systems in Europe and North America were generally equal. After the war, tools and medications were scarce in Germany. Over there, you might get medication for two post-operative days. After that, most people refused further medication, as they were more interested in a homeopathic approach. I didn't give as many sleeping pills there as here, where people seem to be more pampered, and the staff had more materials to work with. When I worked in Switzerland, you'd almost have to force people to take something for pain. They were sturdy, somehow.

When I started as a nursing assistant in Peterborough, there was a patient who needed a bandage changed. The bandage wasn't soiled, but I changed the pad it held. I stood there and rolled up the bandage. I said, "I'm rolling up the bandage." She said, "Oh, no, we don't use them again. We throw them out." I said, "This is not soiled, and it can go back on the same patient." But, no, that wasn't the way it was done. That was my biggest surprise. There was such a waste in Canada. I ended up saving the hospital a lot of money. I didn't cut corners, but I did conserve.

In Europe, the physicians were like gods; in Canada, they were more like colleagues. This was a nice change.

For medical care in Europe, we nurses did a lot of looking after people in a personal way, such as bathing them twice a day, and giving them back rubs to make them comfortable. The care was good. The hours were longer. After the war, everything was not quite the way it had been. In Wels, we worked 24 hours on, and 24 hours off. In Germany you worked 12 hours a day, and the same in Switzerland. There, we did have two hours at noontime for lunch and a rest. We ate lunch fast, and then went to our room and slept.

The atmosphere in Europe was strict—white coat and tie. It was '*Herr Professor*' and '*Herr Doktor;*' you didn't call anybody by their first name. It took me a long time to call doctors in Canada by their first name. There are still people in Peterborough who remember me working at the hospital, and they still call me "Mrs. K" (a shortening of my married name, Kurowski) when I meet them. I was the only one that called people by their family name, and they called me by my family name. If you didn't do that, it somehow lowered the standard, and it wasn't right.

Conversion

I converted to Catholicism officially in 1962. I was taught by a man named Jim Coughlan, with classes at St. Peter's High School on Reid Street in Peterborough. I took instruction because I didn't know enough about it. He instructed me completely, about the bible, and the Eucharist, and the meaning of everything. My confirmation name was Teresa, after Mother Teresa of Calcutta. I was confirmed at St. Peter's.

I didn't have to learn Latin. I didn't understand all the mass in Latin, but I liked it. I still like it.

Somehow Christ's presence was always with you in a church. I noticed a difference in the tradition. In Germany I went mostly the last year to a Catholic church, rather than a Protestant one, even though I worked at a Protestant hospital. We prayed at the hospital, because it was Protestant sisters. When I came here, it was almost that the religious tradition suited me.

I was already concentrated on Catholicism; I was already friendly with it. I felt good about it; at home. It filled a void which I didn't know what is. Somehow, I left the church happier than when I went in. Tadeusz influenced me by his example. I thought there must be something to it, because he was so devoted, and felt so strongly about it, and never wavered. I was obviously in favor of becoming a Catholic. I felt like I was at home there, and that it was where I should be. The Lutheran services had become superficial somehow, and artificial. They didn't give me the same nourishment for my wounded soul. The Catholic readings, the homilies, the whole atmosphere was more interesting than just meditation. It spoke to my soul. I had an empty feeling at the other church; it didn't give me satisfaction for my inner desires. My soul still hadn't healed from the past. It had gone through various hurdles, and it needed to be nourished in the right way.

I liked the ceremonies that were new to me—the kneeling, bowing, bell-ringing, for example. The meaning of the Eucharist—the body and blood of Christ. This just showed to me that there was more respect for the majesty of God. There was new meaning as I began to understand more, as I was taught more. The picture was completed. Many questions were answered.

Becoming Catholic was for me the cream on top. An unknown yearning for something had accumulated in me. When I became a Catholic, it was like a crowning of that yearning; I began a new life. That's the way it felt—I was a new human being. It was a confirmation that I had made the right decision.

I felt good about it, because it was a step in the right direction. It filled a void. There was somehow some emptiness that I felt, before. It gave me a good feeling, and made me happy. I was satisfied with myself, that I had fulfilled my dream. I had started a new life, as a Catholic. I looked at life differently, in many ways. I had always been emotional, and kind to people, but it made me more aware that you always have to be nice. There's an obligation for it, where it had not been before. Christian obligations.

My sister Liselotte married a Catholic man, and she converted beforehand to Catholicism. She became a devoted Catholic. In Europe and Germany, if you don't go to a civil ceremony, you aren't officially married. She went to the city hall, and had the official marriage there. The church wedding was a few days later. She did not live with her husband until she had been married in the church. That's how she embraced Catholicism.

In becoming a Catholic, I did not feel that I had abandoned my family, Lutheranism or my heritage. When I went to church as a child, I didn't look at it the same way as I do as an adult. I'm quite sure my parents would have agreed with my change.

I felt comfortable, and that I had found answers and nourishment for my heart and soul in the Catholic Church. The question had been answered. I had found complete loyalty to the Catholic Church, and was sure that I would practice it to the best of my ability.

When I went into a Catholic church, I immediately found an atmosphere of safety and peace. I sometimes felt surrounded with angels. I felt protected there. Everything in an old church has a special atmosphere. I found I was in another world—not a dream world—where you find comfort, where your conscience clears, where you make a promise to yourself that you want to live up to the standard of the doctrine. This is the way I felt. I felt a feeling of satisfaction after I had gone to church. The emptiness was gone.

I'm still inquisitive about the meaning of the words of scripture. God had (and has) common sense, that's for sure. If you know how to interpret scripture, it's easy to understand God.

I sometimes wish God would speak to me directly, though he never has. Despite that, I have a feeling that I've been constantly guided by God. Even every day in the street, at work and at home, I've been watched over by God and protected. For example, those times that I've almost had a car accident (say when changing lanes when I hadn't even looked!), I thought right away that God was watching over me.

God is not tangible, but it's what you build your faith on. I've had so many examples in my life that I escaped from harm or danger. It hasn't all just been by accident—there has to be a higher force that protected me. Angels, or God, or the Virgin Mary intervened. I never have taken it as being just a coincidence.

Tadeusz was happy that I converted. I knew he would be. He never forced me. He waited for me. He knew that I would learn by his example of being a Catholic. By this alone, his never pushing me by influence or word, I knew he was happy that I had found my faith.

I enjoyed it more and more, and there would eventually be moments when I was in church when I'd feel, "I'm so happy I'm a Catholic."

8. Those Two Nice Husbands

1963 Peterborough, Canada

Marriage

Tadeusz's wife, Jakubina Kurowski, died of cancer in 1962, having never left Poland. He waited for another year, and then he asked me to marry him. When Tadeusz proposed marriage, he said he would like us to spend the rest of our lives together. We knew we would be happy.

When I first came to Canada, his wife was still alive, though she had breast cancer. Every extra penny he had, he still used to buy and send medication to her in Poland. I helped too, once I was earning money. There was a branch of the state-managed Polish bank Pekao in Toronto, just like there had been back in Germany. He would pay in Canadian dollars in Toronto, and the next day they would have the money in Poland. As an example, if a Pole heated their home using coal, they were assigned a quota by the state. If they ran out, it was too bad—they would have to live in a cold house. Tadeusz's family had a big house in the country, because they'd lost their homes in Warsaw, and it needed a lot of coal. (Their parents had built it as a summer home, circa 1900.) If Tadeusz paid for coal for them in Canada, they would get it delivered the next day. If he paid for medication, they got the medication. His wife had a fur coat that was stolen, so we bought a new coat for her. Tadeusz put his son, Andrzej Kurowski, through university with our combined help for tuition. Andrzej later died in a car accident, but Tadeusz's grandson Bartłomieja Kurowski and his mother still live in Poland. I'm in regular contact with them, and have a good relationship with them. I've visited them many times.

When I lived in the residence at the hospital nursing college, I visited Tadeusz, Władysław and his wife. It was sort of dating, but he never made any promise in words about getting married. We knew somehow that we both wanted to be together.

We were married on April 29, 1963 in Idaho, because my soon-to-be brother-in-law was training there. I was 37, and Tadeusz was 53. We had driven there by car from Peterborough. By then I was already Catholic, and we were married in the Catholic Church in Orofino, St. Theresa's. The guests were just Władysław, his wife and their daughter, and a physician friend who acted as a witness. After our small wedding, we went to a restaurant, and that was it. We didn't have much money.

We bought a little house on McDonnel Street in Peterborough. It was a small house with a white-picket fence, but it had a big yard, and after we remodeled the house, it was all nicely done. One of the doctors at the hospital asked me if we had a housewarming. I said, yes, we had just got the oil furnace in that week. He laughed and told me what a 'housewarming' really was. In the late 1960s, the whole area was expropriated when a new police station was built there, so we had to move again.

After his initial tutoring, Tadeusz had applied for a license in health insurance, taking the exam in French because it was his stronger language. However, selling insurance wasn't his forte, so he gave it up. He worked for many years in the medical supply room, as his first job at Peterborough Civic. There was another Polish fellow working with him there, who had been a judge in Poland. The judge couldn't afford to go university for certification in Canada, either.

Later, Tadeusz took an accounting course and became an accountant at the hospital for the staff credit union. He eventually retired due to ill health—prostate cancer—but he still tutored from home.

Sharing

I have always liked dancing, ballroom dancing. Tadeusz and I, we always went to dances, like at the CN Tower in Toronto for New Year's parties. When we were on holidays, we danced anywhere.

He was a religious person, a devoted Catholic. Every book he had, had a cross on it. Whenever we bought a loaf of bread (it wasn't sliced back then), he always made a cross on the bread, and thanked God.

It didn't matter where we were—Fiji, Italy, Hawaii. When we traveled, we always went to church. In Fiji, the priest was barefoot. They had straw mats in the church, and all the people were dressed up. We traveled through France along the Mediterranean to Italy. When we arrived in Milan, we had to wait a few hours in the railroad station one Sunday morning. There was a chapel in the station, and a mass going on, so we didn't miss the mass. Everywhere we went, we went to mass.

We liked to dance. We liked photography. We went to Toronto to the theater: light operas and musicals. We went to what we could afford. Sometimes we had New Year's parties at our house—we invited people, and had a lot of fun. We had a really good social life.

We often visited in Germany—we traveled there a lot. You have to pay a price, when you're far away from friends and family.

Illness

In 1974, he got sick, prostate cancer, and he had radiation treatment. Oh, but he was sick; terribly sick. A urologist in Toronto had recommended radiation, because at that time a prostatectomy was far from perfect. If the bladder was nicked, well, you can't sew up a bladder, so there was that danger. He had 26 radiation treatments.

He stayed at the lodge of Princess Margaret Hospital in Toronto during the week, while he had therapy, and would come home to Peterborough on weekends. On Friday, volunteers drove people home. He'd arrive Friday evening, and be picked up again Monday morning. He'd spend the whole weekend in bed. He couldn't eat, couldn't even drink water. He couldn't have coffee, which he had loved, because the smell nauseated him. Because I was a nurse, and I was on the intravenous (IV) team when I worked in the operating room, I asked permission to get IV solution and equipment. The whole weekend, I would have him on the IV. We didn't have an IV stand, so I hung the solution bag up on the curtain rod. At least over the weekend, he was well hydrated.

We went to Lourdes, in France, for a week during that time. I'm sure it helped him. We went every day to the healing mass in the square, and we did the Stations of the Cross. We thanked God, and felt good, even comfortable about it. The whole town is geared toward pilgrimage—everyone in the hotels is there as a pilgrim. The whole atmosphere was for praying.

It took him a while, but he did recover afterward. Then it was good, and he persisted again with tutoring. About ten years later, in 1984, he noticed a lump on his neck. It was diagnosed as lymphoma. I sent him to the doctor. A malignant lump is hard, but this one was movable. It was in a strange place, even for a fatty lump. It was removed, and underneath was a cancerous lymph node. He lived for only about six more weeks. He soon lost his appetite, and went down quickly.

I took a leave of absence from my work. He was in St. Joseph's Hospital in Peterborough. I lived and slept and ate with him in his room for the entire six weeks. I slept in reclining chair, and stayed with him day and night. I didn't even leave him for 20 minutes, because I felt better with him. People told me I should go out for an hour, or take a rest. I said, "No, I'll feel better if I am with him." I was with him when he died. I never left him. For the whole, entire six weeks I stayed with him, day and night.

Before he died, and he still had his mental faculties, he dictated to me letters of goodbye and farewell to his friends. This was hard for me. He asked them to look after me, if they could. He wanted to come home one more time, and we tried, but it was too painful for him to sit up and lie down. We took him back to the hospital.

God was with us. He gave me the strength to be with Tadeusz all the time. I prayed with him every night, until I couldn't hear Tadeusz speaking any more. When he died, I prayed right away. When the priest came, and the sisters came, we had a lot of religious support. God was always with him. He died on a Saturday, July 27, 1985, at the age of 75.

Before his death, he told me his wish: "When I'm in my coffin, I want to you put a white cloth and three red roses in my arms. The first rose is for God, the second rose is for my mother, and the third rose is for you." I had to cry. You can see what kind of man he was. I did this, of course. White and red are the colors of the Polish flag.

He was cremated, and I planned to take the ashes to Poland. However, there was the nuclear accident at Chernobyl in the Soviet Union early in 1986, so I postponed it for a year. I didn't want to go the same year, with the fallout of all the radioactive materials. I went through the complete, honest and official way, although people wondered why I didn't just take the ashes in a container in my purse without telling anyone. I wrote to the Governor-General of Canada, and signed my husband's ashes out of the country. I went to the Polish consulate, and they told me what I had to do: I would need a copper urn, and a plastic box with the ashes inside. It was sealed in the Polish consulate. I carried his ashes in my lap on the trip, and I had another funeral for him in Poland. We buried his ashes out in the country where his family had their house, near where his mother and an aunt were buried. The town is in the province of Łódź, just a few kilometers from the city of Łódź, and is called Szczawin. His father was buried in Warsaw.

After his death, I kept on working, though I needed counseling. I was by myself, with no relatives. I was heartbroken. My heart was bleeding. I cried anywhere, even in the street. I was depressed, very depressed. I'd come home crying—oh my.

The counseling helped. The first thing the counselor said was that I had to say goodbye to my husband. I said, "No way." You have to go through a process, and slowly get better and better. If I had met my eventual second husband that year, I wouldn't have been ready.

Time gives healing, but you don't forget. When you work, it's a good thing, because you don't have much time to think about it. I had a hard road for a while having to console patients and make them comfortable, because I needed to be consoled.

I had many friends we had chummed around with. Some never phoned, never asked about how I was managing. I had other good friends that did, though, did inquire about it. You wonder: why, why? This is just the way people are, so you had to put up with it.

I was head nurse for ear, nose and throat surgery during the time when I was grieving. In the surgical area, there were always patients lying on stretchers in the hallway, waiting for various operations. I had to go down that corridor to get an instrument that a surgeon asked for from a storage room. I was going by in a hurry, when I noticed one of the patients, a woman, was crying. She wasn't my patient. Something was telling me there was something wrong here, so I stopped and asked her why she was crying. Something was telling me to help—God's intervention—and meantime my colleagues were shouting out to me, "Where is Brigitte?" I asked the woman, "What are you afraid of?" She said, "I don't want to lose my baby."

I asked her who told her she had to lose her baby, and told her she had the right to change her mind. She said, "I can? They're prepared and waiting for me." I told her it didn't mean a thing; she could change her mind, and if she didn't want to lose her baby she didn't have to. I took my time, and I told her I would get her physician.

He came out, and the next thing I knew the patient was off the floor, and she didn't abort her baby. I had to return to my operating team. If I hadn't taken the time to stop, because I was in a rush, I wouldn't have been able to help. She got thinking while she was lying there.

1988 Peterborough, Canada

Then I met my second husband.

One Sunday afternoon, in June of 1988, I read in the local newspaper that there was a former school teacher who wanted to form a singles' club. Once a year, they would have a weekend where people who were divorced or single or widowed could get together. They could golf, or play cards and in the evening, dance. I thought it sounded interesting. Dancing. I liked that.

I forgot all about it until one day three weeks later, when I was cutting the grass on a Saturday afternoon. All of a sudden it came into my mind that I hadn't phoned yet about the singles' club. I phoned, and it so happened that the former teacher was there. He told me what it was all about, and what they wanted to do. I told him I was mainly interested in dancing. He said this was just what he particularly wanted to teach people about—waltz, foxtrot, and tango. He said he knew a man who had recently lost his wife. He was originally from England, his name was Alan Wilson, and he was a particularly adept social ballroom dancer. He lived out on Chemong Lake, just north of the city. The instructor had Alan's phone number, and suggested I call some time.

I thought, "Why wait for some time?" So I called him right away. He was hard to get, because after his wife died he was always out with friends or traveling on his motorcycle or driving his car. He had built his own motorcycle when he was 14 years old. Fortunately, this time he was home, and I told him why I was calling. He said he wanted to meet me. And I said I wanted to meet him. He asked if half an hour would be enough. Sure!

I went into the house and spruced myself up a little bit (remember, I had been cutting the lawn). Here he comes, in his car. I received him on the terrace. I offered him a drink. He said, yes, he would have a cup of tea—typically English. So we had the cup of tea.

He told me the plan for the club was for two nights of performance, a Saturday and Sunday, where people would perform dancing and music. We two would be dancing. We'd have to perform two dances.

He got up, took me in arms, swung me around, and said, "Oh, yes. You're flexible."

He suggested we rent a room somewhere to do our practicing. He wanted to prepare five dances for demonstration. As it was, I had a big basement—one half was for utilities and laundry, and the other half was a recreation room. It was air conditioned, too. He said it would do just fine, though we would have to cut our steps a little bit shorter than normal, but it would do.

We practiced our five dances every night for about three weeks: a tango, a cha-cha, a Viennese waltz, an English waltz and a rhumba. We practiced, and we performed for the two nights. One was at the Rock Haven hotel just at the outskirts of the city, and the other was at a hall in the nearby village of Keene. It wasn't a competition; we just performed for the people who came out for the singles' night. There were about thirty people, from near and far, who watched us. Afterward, there was social dancing and food and drink.

Before the weekend was out, the teacher suggested we choose a date for next year when we could do this again. In order to do that, we'd have to reserve a room, and it would mean we'd have to each pay about $60. Not everyone paid, and so the whole thing fell apart.

That was the end of the dancing club. But that was how Alan and I started.

Alan used to go back to England every year, even when his wife was still alive, and had done so for twenty-seven consecutive years. He was close to his family, his brothers and sisters. His next trip had been set for one week's time. He said if he had met me earlier, he wouldn't have gone to England. So, you can see the chemistry was already working a little bit.

I told him he'd better go, and off he went. He came in the morning of his flight to say goodbye. Two days later, the phone rang at six o'clock in the morning. I knew it would be him, and it was. He phoned me every second day from England. He wrote me letters. It grew and grew to where he was missing me. You know how it is.

✼ ✼ ✼

When he came back, it was two months later. It was September, 1988, and happened to be my 63rd birthday. He proposed to me, and gave me a diamond ring. That evening, I was on emergency call at the hospital. An hour after he gave me the ring, I was called there to assist at an operation. Ah, well.

We talked about it. He wondered what we were waiting for. So, we got married the following year, on February 11, 1989. I was not yet 64, and Alan was 76.

After we got married, I retired a year early—what was the point in waiting?

He asked where we should live. I said that when I was on call during the night, it would be further from where he lived in Bridgenorth, so I would prefer to live in my house. He was amenable, and said he'd sell his house.

When Alan and I were planning our wedding, I said it was funny going from a Polish name to an English one. He said 'Kurowski-Wilson' had kind of a nice ring to it, and asked if I would like to call myself that. I had no reason not to. He said fine. One day he said he had gone to city hall and had his own name changed, also to Kurowski-Wilson. So we were both married with that name. He said, "There, I've changed my name." I said I hoped he didn't mind, and he said he did not at all. The license plate on my car still shows our combination: AKW • BKW.

We never had any problems. We liked the same things, like photography and traveling. He was enthusiastic about everything.

Alan belonged to Mark Street United Church. Once we knew each other, he went with me to St. Peter's Catholic Church. We were married in the United church, because he would otherwise have had to take a six months' course in Catholic catechism. We were married by Reverend Root. I stayed a Catholic, and he went with me to the Catholic church, and I went with him once a month to his church.

He was born in Bradford, England, in 1913. He had a brother and four sisters. When the war started, he enlisted. They needed engineers. The British had an underground airplane factory between Bradford and Leeds, and they told him they'd rather he worked as an electrical engineer there than fight as a soldier somewhere else.

After the war was over, Lord Beaverbrook promoted the idea of sending professionals to Canada. The boys who belonged to the farm and had worked in the factories, he wanted them to go back to the farm. Alan had a job waiting for him at the General Electric generator plant in Peterborough. He arrived in the winter time, and he and his wife bought a house. Eventually, he and his wife spent winters in Florida, living in a trailer park there.

His wife began to get sick, having heart attacks and cardiac arrests. He retired three years early to look after her. With her medical care, it became too expensive to stay in Florida, so they sold their trailer and stayed in Canada year-round. As well as her heart problems, she developed breast cancer and a brain tumor before her death. He had lost his wife a year before Tadeusz died.

Both my husbands dressed perfectly. They both brought me flowers. It was like a continuation from the Tadeusz to Alan. The only difference was that my first husband was meticulous in everything. For example, after he used his handkerchief, he would fold it up neatly, as it was before. My second husband would just crumple it up and put it in his pocket.

They were both good and kind. My first husband called me 'my angel,' and my second husband called me 'my love' (as the English do).

Alan believed in God, and was an elder at his church. We both were believers. I asked the Catholic bishop if Alan could come with me to church. He said if Alan was a Christian, it was fine. We didn't really discuss religion as such.

Alan was a gentleman. He was a Kiwanian, a member of a local men's charity organization, and he canvassed for all sorts of other charities. He helped every year with collecting for the Salvation Army's Christmas hampers. He and first wife were recommended by the local Member of Parliament for recognition for their extensive charity work, and they were invited to a tea party of the Queen's at Buckingham Palace in recognition. One of his cousins drove them there in a Rolls Royce.

※ ※ ※

Alan was a Type II diabetic, but at first didn't know he had any signs, and he didn't know for how long he had diabetes before that.

When he was younger, he often drank tea with a lot of sugar in it. His wife attended a diabetic clinic herself, and one time when he was there he asked the staff if they would mind measuring his blood sugar. They discovered he was a Type II diabetic. Initially he was treated with diet and pills, but it got so bad he went on insulin and eventually his kidneys shut down. He went on dialysis but then after a time it didn't work anymore, either.

He was given one week to live, and they wanted to take him to a rehabilitation center. I refused, took him home, and he lived for seven more weeks. We prayed every night together, before he went to sleep. One prayer I learned from him was, "As I go down to sleep, pray thee Lord my soul to keep. Should I die before I wake, pray thee Lord my soul to keep." I prayed the 'Our Father' and the 'Hail Mary,' and he prayed those with me.

Alan was still alive when I first heard a local Catholic priest from Nigeria, Father Stan Chu Ilo, at a mass at St. Peter's. My husband said he was an interesting man, and that he would like to meet him. He suggested we invite him to our home, which we did. He helped my husband tremendously as he was dying.

Alan died on June 23, 2003.

9. Two Tunics to Share

2003 Peterborough, Canada

Since then, I'm alone.

With both my dear husbands, we had always done things together, and led lively lives; we liked to travel. I'm an outgoing person, so being with people is important. Now, I involve myself with a lot of volunteer work. I read in a church three times a week; I sing in a choir; I dance—ballroom dancing, line dancing. My second husband and I, we danced every week in Toronto, ballroom dancing with a real instructor. I play in a band, and belong to the Catholic Women's League—we do things there. I am involved, and I work for charity as much as I can. It's still a daily struggle to be on my own, because all my relatives are still over there in Europe. Of course, I have wonderful friends.

I keep busy.

With being a nurse all my life, you're always giving, and it becomes your nature. When I met my first husband, I helped him support his wife and son with the cost of her medications when she was sick in Poland. Despite all the money I lost, and all the people of Germany lost, after the war, life (God) gave me a chance to get back on my feet. It wasn't just by sheer luck or determination. By then, I already had a spiritual feeling that it was the right thing to do, to help. I never blink an eye about giving. It makes me feel good to help, to give something. If someone needed money, I could give it to them, knowing they needed it more than I did. To me, this is spiritual intervention. My first husband, Tadeusz, as a good Catholic was always open to giving. My second husband, Alan, was so involved with raising money for different charities and causes. I've always been around people who willingly and happily help others.

So, this is what I keep doing. It gives me joy. It's rewarding to see that you can make a difference.

Father Stan Chu Ilo told Alan and I about his charity, and we gave him a check right there. Later, I joined the *Canadian Samaritans for Africa* group, and Father Stan mentioned they had some building projects planned in Nigeria. He invited me to accompany him there, and when I went I saw the real need of the people there. I gave money to help to rebuild, and it's kept going and going.

I was accustomed to sharing and giving all my life, whether money, or possessions, or my personal help. I learned this from my parents. In Germany in the early 1930s, before Hitler came to power, there was widespread unemployment. People who were out of work came every day to my parents for food and help, because my father as a schoolteacher was a social focal point. They had the maid cook for these people, with a typical dish being *Eintopf* (literally, one pot), with vegetables, meat and potatoes. When people came, my mother would give it out.

❋ ❋ ❋

Another charity I've been involved with based in Canada is Friends of Honduran Children. Under their auspices, I went with a local physician, Hardy Friesen, and a medical brigade to Honduras for twelve days, to help people who have no access to medical services. Volunteers pay everything themselves to get there.

The original trip was put together by a Peterborough dentist, Jim McCallum. The people who live in remote mountain villages have no doctors or dentists, in part because they live far away. These medical brigade trips were formed, typically consisting of about 20 people.

The one I went with included two dentists from Peterborough and four physicians, with the balance being active and retired nurses, capable all.

We were all volunteers, and I was the oldest in our group. For months beforehand, we worked every week packaging, unpackaging and repackaging—we needed to cut down the size and weight of the supplies we were bringing. For example, we removed medicine capsules that were originally packaged in little pouches, transferring them to bottles. For the airplane trip, each person had to carry with them 50 pounds of medication and supplies in a big hockey equipment bag. The supplies were donated by pharmaceutical companies and physicians' offices, and we had to check everything for expiry dates.

Three groups went at different times, organized by Dr. Friesen. Dr. Holmes led my group. We paid for our own flight to Honduras, and were housed at a local community hall there where we slept in bunk beds. We loaded equipment, supplies and medicine on trucks every morning, and drove for about 90 minutes to a remote village. Our convoy went down between the mountains, and up through rugged areas, through creeks. We started seeing patients at ten in the morning. They were already lined up when we got there. Some had walked for hours to get there, some of those without shoes.

We set up a make-shift clinic. There were four rooms, one for each of our physicians. None of our patients spoke English, so each physician had to have a Spanish translator with them. We had a makeshift pharmacy. We had a triage nurse. Besides medications, we had brought clothes and eyeglasses. Once we had everything set up, we started to see the patients.

Some patients had minor surgery on the spot, though we could not do anything that was complicated. If needed, they were given a prescription for our pharmacy, and they received multivitamins. We treated whatever we could—gastrointestinal, heart problems, high blood pressure. They gave us a healthy lunch, and we worked until four o'clock. Then we put everything back on the trucks, drove back to our base, and unpacked everything again. That evening, we talked about our experiences, and had a briefing on the plans for the next day. This went on for seven days, every day at a new place.

We visited some homes as well. They were poor, with piles of rocks used for cooking. They of course had no mattresses. Children would be lying on the ground in a pile of dirty clothes. We had brought some mattresses with us, which we were able to give them.

We went in February, 2007. It was a tiring journey, but thoroughly rewarding. We felt good, knowing that we had helped them. I looked after handing out the hundreds of donated prescription eyeglasses that we had brought with us. I tried them all on with the people, and it was fun. I'd try different pairs of glasses on them, working to find just the right prescription. Once we found it, they would be so happy, men and women. "Bravo, bravo!" they'd say, patting us on the shoulder.

We brought children's shoes, and we'd let them pick out which ones they wanted. One young girl had come barefoot from the mountains with her mother, and she picked out shiny black patent leather party shoes. She liked them, even though they were absolutely unsuitable for her region.

It was fun. The people were nice; we loved them. Our patients showed their appreciation with their hugs, handshakes and smiles. In the evening everyone was glad, because we knew that we were helping them. It was an absolute joy.

After we were all unpacked each night we'd have supper and then our briefing. We'd have to get up early the next morning. We were just talking about this patient or that one. The dentist could only pull teeth, and because there was no local electricity supply they used flashlights when they looked into the patients' mouths. An injection of anesthetic would be needed before a tooth could be pulled. Some children were better than some of the adults, who were chickens!

I arranged a medical brigade to go to Nigeria in 2011. It was all set and ready to go, including accommodation there for our team which was arranged by a Nigerian bishop. Unfortunately, shortly before we were to leave, there was some terrorist activity there against Westerners. Our trip was canceled, and that ended my dream to get medical aid to Nigeria. They are poor there, too, and many can't afford or can't get to a physician.

Friends of Honduran Children are now organizing building brigades to Honduras, to enlarge orphanages to help with the significant numbers of orphaned children there. I still help with the packing for them for their medical brigades, and with their fundraisers. The flights and missions are too long for me now, though I would love to be able to go.

❈ ❈ ❈

Once Father Stan told me about problems in Nigeria, how when he was a young boy they had to transport water from a lake, because they had no supply immediately at hand, I was ready immediately to help. The village supply of drinking water was contaminated, and there were flies that bit people and led to blindness. He had formed a charity, and invited me to go with him to Nigeria. There was a cook who attended St. Peter's as well at the time, and she agreed to go.

In Nigeria, I met Father Stan's parents, and was introduced to various women's groups. We saw firsthand what they needed; first of all was fresh water, so a well needed be built. An American charitable organization, "Engineers Without Borders," was contacted and they agreed to help. However, the terrain would have required a 400 foot bore hole, and a transformer and a pump, and storage tanks. People would have been able to bring their containers to get fresh water. However, the original estimate of $5,000 grew to $20,000.

There's a lake fed by a small river. It's contaminated—people do their washing, and the run-off pollutes the water. Cassava is a local food staple; before it can be eaten, it needs to be processed by soaking in water to remove a toxin, which also leads to pollution. They needed a new, reliable source of fresh water. With a supply connection to the women's building, they could use it to wash the cassava and use the residue for something else. This would give them a job, and an income.

There was also a school that needed a roof on it.

I've put some collection boxes in various businesses around town, where patrons can put in coins. Every little bit helps. There's a couple in the apartment building I live in who give a monthly donation. People around here sometimes have a tendency to say they only support local charities, so sometimes we have trouble.

I went to Nigeria a second time in 2008, and I laid the cornerstone for the women's center there. Father Stan asked us if we would like to go, so we went on the spur of the moment. It was easy to decide to go again. That second time, we stayed in Father Stan's family's compound. The first time, I stayed with nuns in a cloister. We went in the spring for two weeks, once the monsoon season was over. I have a lot of friends there now; I'm good friends with Father Stan's parents. They told me I'm now part of their family, which is good because I don't have any family here.

We met Father Alex, from Uganda. He's in charge of a boys' school there. They needed an irrigation system there because they grow their own vegetables. There's been a drought there recently. *Canadian Samaritans for Africa*, of which I'm a board member, has an agenda for our charity, and at the moment we're concentrating on Uganda. I sponsored Father Anthony Ezeonwueme to come to Canada for a trip. He is now at a parish in Canada, as a priest in the Diocese of Peterborough.

Nigeria is delightful; the people are so happy. Going to church is the main event of the week, and they go there beautifully dressed. You can hear a group of women walking through the grass to the church. The children are quiet and respectful in church, the boys on one side and the girls on the other. The mass is a pleasure. The music is wonderful, with the drums and the choir. There is a happiness, somehow. Everybody sings. There is no collection; instead they bring their own donations. They bring food—they may bring a live goat. People enjoy themselves.

They dance on Sunday afternoon. I danced with them, and when you dance they put money on your forehead. I left the money on the floor, of course, and someone else collected it. They enjoyed themselves so much, just being together. It was delightful, and they stole my heart.

The people act as if they know you. They hug everybody. I began to hug everybody, too. They have beautiful clothes—they look better dressed than the richest people in the Western world. When I was in Jamaica, at church the girls had flowers braided into their hair, and nice clothes on. I just love to go to other countries, because they are so interesting to see.

Nigeria is a happy place. Since my second husband died, I've had nobody. Over there, they would never leave you alone. They would stay with you for the grieving time. There is such togetherness. Families help each other. Neighbors help each other.

I love Nigeria. I wish I could go again, but it is dangerous at the moment. Those terrorists are active now, and there's uncertainty about where and when they'll strike. Abuja is the capital, and a beautiful city. As soon as you leave the city, the country roads are generally not paved, and if they are it's all broken up. In the city, the roads are alright. In the villages, there is more of a personal touch than there is in the cities. Everyone knows each other, and everyone helps each other. There is a contrast there, too.

People are somehow happy, even if they have nothing. I told them that we Westerners could learn something from them. Here in the West, we are unhappy for having everything. That's why it's my mission to help them with whatever I can, as long as I can.

The poverty in Nigeria is everywhere. There is no infrastructure. There's garbage on the road, and nobody picks it up. In Canada, the poor people are richer than people generally in Nigeria. Canadians have food banks and welfare; there is no such thing in Nigeria. I saw a woman and two children there sitting on the sidewalk. One of the children had a cleft palate. It was in the evening, and you could see they had no place to go. They had no help whatsoever.

In our medical brigade Honduras, there was nothing religious at all. You just worked there, and that was it. I did my prayers every morning and at night, alone, but there was nothing done as a group. We didn't go to a church; that wasn't part of the meaning of the trip. You just went there to look after the patients, there was nothing connected with the church.

In Nigeria, the people's faith permeates the whole area. You get caught in it, and you can feel their devotion to God. The people were in contact with God; you could sense their deep faith because they showed it in all their actions. Our car broke down one day, and we were immediately surrounded by people who were trying to help. In the church, the atmosphere is much different than it is here. Everyone is so happy, and you can feel that God is present there in the human bodies.

You never know. Is it because of the priest? Is it because of the way church is conducted? Is it because of being together with your neighbors, worshipping the same? Is it like the Germans and Nazism, carried away in the moment? Or is it all the time like that? It's hard to determine. I was swept away by the enthusiasm of the people, during those moments at church. I was enchanted. There was complete participation by the people, whereas in Canada a lot of people don't even sing. The Nigerians are proud of being a community, and being together, and helping each other. They all seemed to feel the same.

I certainly felt like I'd been in a church. This is what I missed when I came back to Canada. No church bells. No signal that something was going to happen. Sometimes those external things influence your emotions.

I just wish the government of Nigeria wasn't so corrupt. They have a lot of oil wealth, but the government is corrupt. The people have survived, but on their own. They know how to help themselves, with their own ingenuity. The people are resigned to the notion that they will always be poor, and they try to live their lives the best they can. They know about modern technology—television, computers—from the Western world, especially the young people, but they know this is the way it is. They are so grateful for any help they receive, so for me it's twice the reward for anything I can give them to better their lives. It's my biggest joy. If I won a lottery, I'd go there and help them with so many things: building schools, building hospitals, improving infrastructure, making their lives better.

I don't know how they are when they're at their homes, but when they're out together, they seem happy. When we went to a village to visit some relatives of one of the priests, everyone came out, smiling and happy. They greet you as if you're an old friend. They have a wonderful attitude. They could be sad all the time, suffering under their hardship, but that's not the way they are.

If they suddenly had more material wealth, it would be a real change for them. I don't know if they would be spoiled like we are. A lot of them have cellphones, because there's no land-line telephone system. The Western people have been spoiled because people want more and more and more, and they get more and more and more. If children don't have electronic toys to play with, they don't know what to do. When my parents were still alive, we played games together. Now, children feel bored without technology. Some of them don't seem to be able to think for themselves any more.

Despite that, there are still young people who want to do things. And they will.

10. Looking Back, and Ahead

My Family

Neither my mother nor my father had many relatives. Our family has shrunk, and I am the last one of my generation.

My sister Liselotte and her husband Josef had two daughters and one son. One daughter, Ursula, lives in Germany, as well as her son, Stefan. (Stefan was born 11 years after Suzanne, just like my sister Liselotte was ten years after me.) The second daughter, Suzanne, lives in Italy, married to an Italian. For the last two years, Suzanne's husband has been slowly dying of ALS.

My brother Hans had one son, Hans-Peter; he and his wife have no children. He's a high school and karate teacher; he has a black belt in karate, and has judged in South America many times. He's also a musician—where he lives, in Schwäbisch Hall in Germany, there's a church with lot of wide steps. Every day, during the summer, they perform opera and plays on the steps, with hardly any makeup or props. They all sing and perform on the steps, and Hans-Peter plays various instruments in the orchestra.

I think about both of my brothers, and my sister, many times. Sometimes I think: I have it behind me, because I lost my parents and now I don't have to worry. If they hadn't died, I probably wouldn't have ended up in Canada to begin with. You have to face it when you're older. Sometimes I wonder what we could have done together if they had all lived, how nice it would have been. But I don't have to face their deaths anymore, and they don't have to face mine. There are pros and cons. Before I retired, I would see how a son or daughter would sit beside their sick parent in the emergency department. I would think what a worry it was for them.

I was the more emotional sibling. My oldest brother actually was too, but he concealed everything. He could never talk about anything. I tried asking him several questions after our parents died, after telling him I had so many questions. But if I asked him something about any incident, even later on, he'd say, "Brigitte. Don't bring up the past again. It's too painful."

The distance and separation between North America and Europe somehow brought my sister and me closer, because every time when I travelled to Germany and visited her, we knew what we meant to each other. We enjoyed each other tremendously.

* * *

My nephew Hans-Peter, and others of his age born after the war, said they have tasted freedom and freedom of expression. He says there's no way that his generation will be brainwashed like we were. There might be another dictatorship, but the people will never allow themselves to be taken in. He says they're tired of being blamed for what we did, and that they would have done things differently if they had been in the same situation. He wonders how you could listen to just one person, for example. They weren't there, though, and they don't know how powerful he was. But I don' think it can happen again. There are so-called Nazi sympathizers now, but they are mostly former East German citizens who were brought up under the Russian dictatorship. Now they are unemployed and disillusioned. They don't have a job or education. There are just pockets of them, and they demonstrate just to make a nuisance. There is no danger, unless perhaps there is another dramatic economic breakdown.

Struggles

Before my parents died, my family's lives were full of blessings, joy and happiness. We had to appreciate what we had, but we had a carefree life. It ended that one day, and brought me into the reality of a stressful world. My childhood was gone in no time, and I grew up in a hurry.

After my parents were gone, I felt lost. I knew that I had to it myself, on my own, that I'd have to find the best way. I deliberately chose people to be with who I knew would have a good influence on me, but to some extent good people just came into my life. I'd have to find a profession, and look after myself and my future.

After my parents died, I was numb, completely numb. Everything was new to me. I had to, all of a sudden, make my own decisions and fight for myself. I had to wake up out of my dreamland, and get back into the reality, do something for myself.

We lost so many mementoes. My father painted portraits of all of us; we had to sit for him every year. He used the same frame, just putting in the new portrait. Everything we had before the war was gone after the war. There was nothing.

The absence of the love of my parents, and the security they gave me, and the protection they gave me, I found now in friends who came into my life without me doing anything. I did not ask for any help establishing myself in the world—I had to do it myself. I did not give up. I was close to giving up at several points. But I chose to keep on going, and make something of my life.

When my brothers had to go off to war, it was another tragedy. I was even more lost, even more by myself. I was in a permanent state of shock. Nothing was real. Only later, when I was in the group of girls at the boarding school, then I slowly, slowly came out of it. My emotions went back to normal reactions. It was a sad time for me. Very sad. Completely lost. I thought there would be no end to it. No help. No psychiatric or psychological help. No counseling. I had to go through all of it by myself. The only friends I had were my nursing colleagues.

When I came back to Germany from Austria, and I was a refugee in my own country, it was traumatic. Everything around me was destroyed. There was no contact with my family; I didn't know who was still alive. Sleeping every night in a refugee camp. People with lice. You couldn't take a bath, or anything. I was absolutely without any hope. I thought I'd end up like other refugees; I didn't know what was going to happen. This was a hopeless situation, when I thought I'd go and take my own life. I thought it would be better than just stumbling between refugee camps.

I ended up doing everything on my own, because I knew this was no life, I had to improve my life, I had to get somewhere, I had to do something about my life, there wasn't anyone else who could help me. Mine is a story of survival.

Everything seemed to be against me; there was nothing easy to achieve. If you fall down, you have to find the strength to get up and get going.

I started out with $35 a month in Canada. I never asked for anything. I never asked for help. There was help, though; I paid my way over here, and there had to be a guarantee that I would not become a burden to the state, which I didn't. I built right away. I studied hard. I got my nursing degree here, so I could function and not be a burden.

I did it alone.

***

But not quite.
God is an important part of my story.

The tragedy of my early life robbed me of childhood, and made me grow up fast. I realized that largely in the absence of the love and friendship of people. Later on, God came into my life, and I saw that everything is designed or ordered by God alone. Through my whole journey until now, I've had a guardian angel watching over me. Everything is nothing but a gift from God.

I know my father was spiritual, very spiritual. So was my grandfather whom I never met, his father. They were a spiritual, Christian family. I think that's what kept my father alive. Now that I'm more mature, I have so many questions. Right after I lost my parents, suddenly there came into my mind questions I'd never asked before. When you're a child, you don't realize life won't go on forever. After they were gone, I realized it was forever, and eternity never ends. They'd never come back. Quite often, even now, I think I should let my brother know some news, but he's gone.

What really sowed the seed for me to become a Catholic was when I was at the hospital in Wels. I felt so safe at that hospital. I felt comfortable, protected, like I belonged to somebody.

After my second husband's death, I was badly hurt by some people, but I could forgive them. God is my guide, and I realize through God I experience all of the love, and I give the love back, and you have to be able to forgive people, and to nourish your friends. Be giving, absolutely giving, helping—open your heart to others, to other people's needs. My heart is in Africa. Poor people here are rich in comparison to those in Africa.

Love and forgiveness and nurturing your friends and compassion are important. The main thing is to love and be forgiving.

It must have all been with God's intervention, that I had the strength, and maybe the good judgment, to fulfill what my goal was, which was to get a job and a profession where I could support myself.

Never give up. There is always hope. God helps you. If you're down, somebody might help you. Don't refuse the help, but if you don't have any help, God will help you, and you will have the strength.

Never forget this. For me, it was God's work. If it doesn't work out, then it was meant to be that way. At least people will say about you, "She was a doer. She didn't give up."

Appendix A: Timelines of the World Wars

Year	Events
1914	Assassination in Sarajevo of Archduke Franz-Ferdinand of the Austro-Hungarian Empire, in June, leading to the formal outbreak of World War One (August 1)
1917	Russian Revolutions, leading to the formation of the Soviet Union in 1922
1918	World War One armistice (November 11)
1923	Appearance of Hitler in Munich *putsch* (coup attempt)
1929	Stock market crash, with ensuing economic depression
1933	Hitler becomes German chancellor after Nazi party electoral victory
1938	Austrian *Anschluss* (joining) with Germany (March 12); Czechoslovakia cedes Sudetenland to Germany (September 30)
1939	World War Two begins: German-Soviet pact (August 23); German invasion of Poland (September 1); declaration of war on Germany by France, Britain and other countries (September 3)
1941	German invasion of the Soviet Union (June 22)
1943	Bombing of Germany and invasion of Italy by the Allies
1944	Invasion of Normandy, France by the Allies (June 6)
1945	Suicide of Adolf Hitler (April 30); end of World War Two in Europe (May 7) and Asia (September 2)

Appendix B: World War One Timeline of Johannes Speidel

Date	Location	Approximate distance from last location (km)
	Heilbronn, Germany	—
September, 1914	Argonne Forest	400
	Bar-le-Duc	50
	Castres	900
September, 1915	Cordes	70
1916	Castres	70
	Augmontel, Mazamet, Montagne Noire	10
	Montauban	100
July, 1916	Valence	500
	Romans-sur-Isère	20
	Lyon	100
	Villeurbanne	10
	Romans-sur-Isère	100
Spring, 1917	Séchilienne/Grenoble	100
April, 1917	La Mure	30
	Ribiers/Sisteron	100
	La Bâtie-Neuve	50
	Gap	1
	Marseille	200
	Sainte-Tulle	100
	Carpiagne	100
	Paris	800
	Étampes	60
	Rouen	200
December, 1918	Croisset	7
	Dieppe	60
	Dunkirk	200
	La Madeleine/Lille	80
	Anor/Fourmies	130
December, 1919	Aulnoye	40
February, 1920	Heilbronn, Germany	500

Total ~5,000 km

Appendix C: Maps

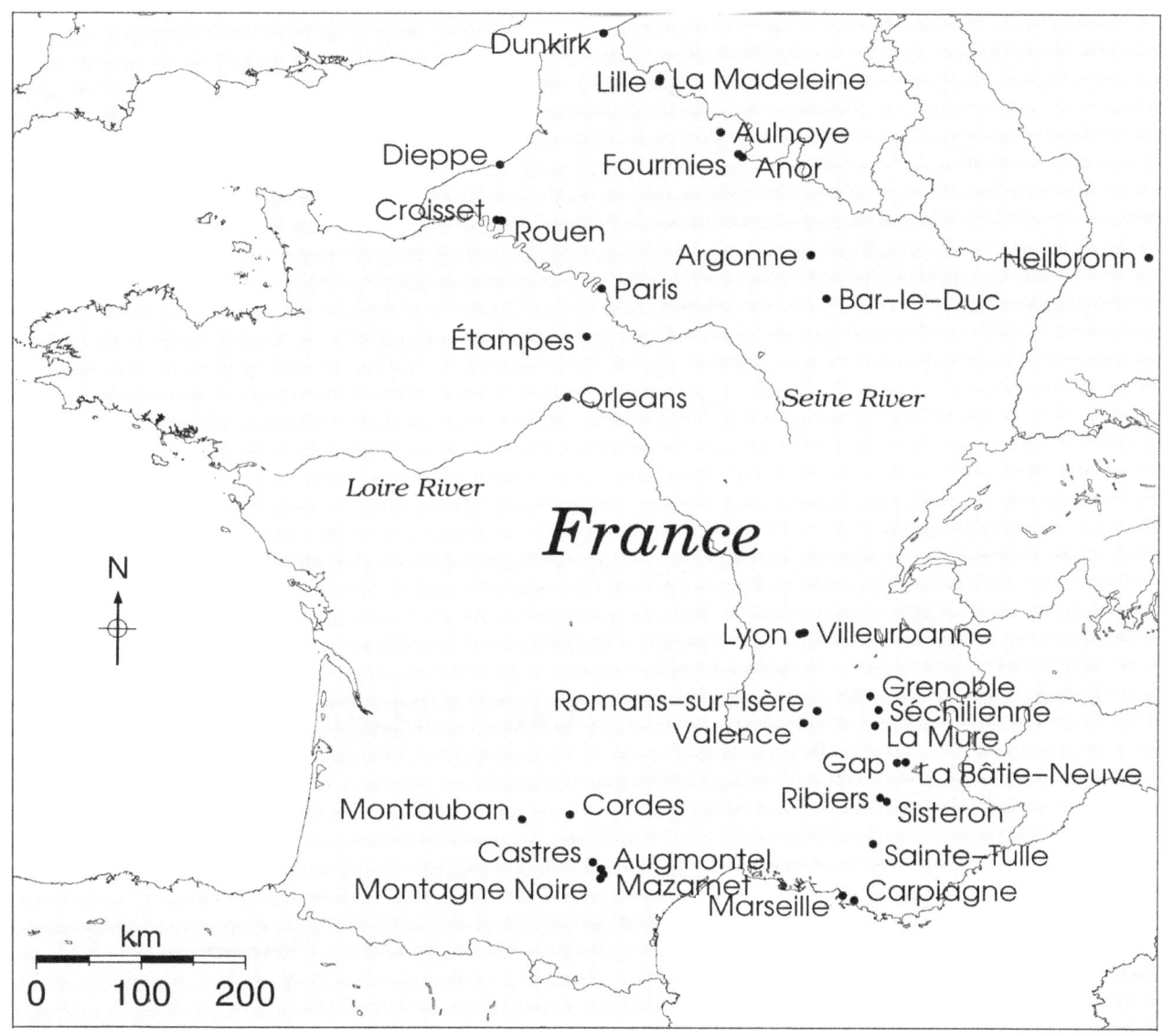

Map 1 Locations cited in Johannes Speidel's World War One autobiography

Map 2 German towns of Brigitte Kurowski-Wilson's childhood

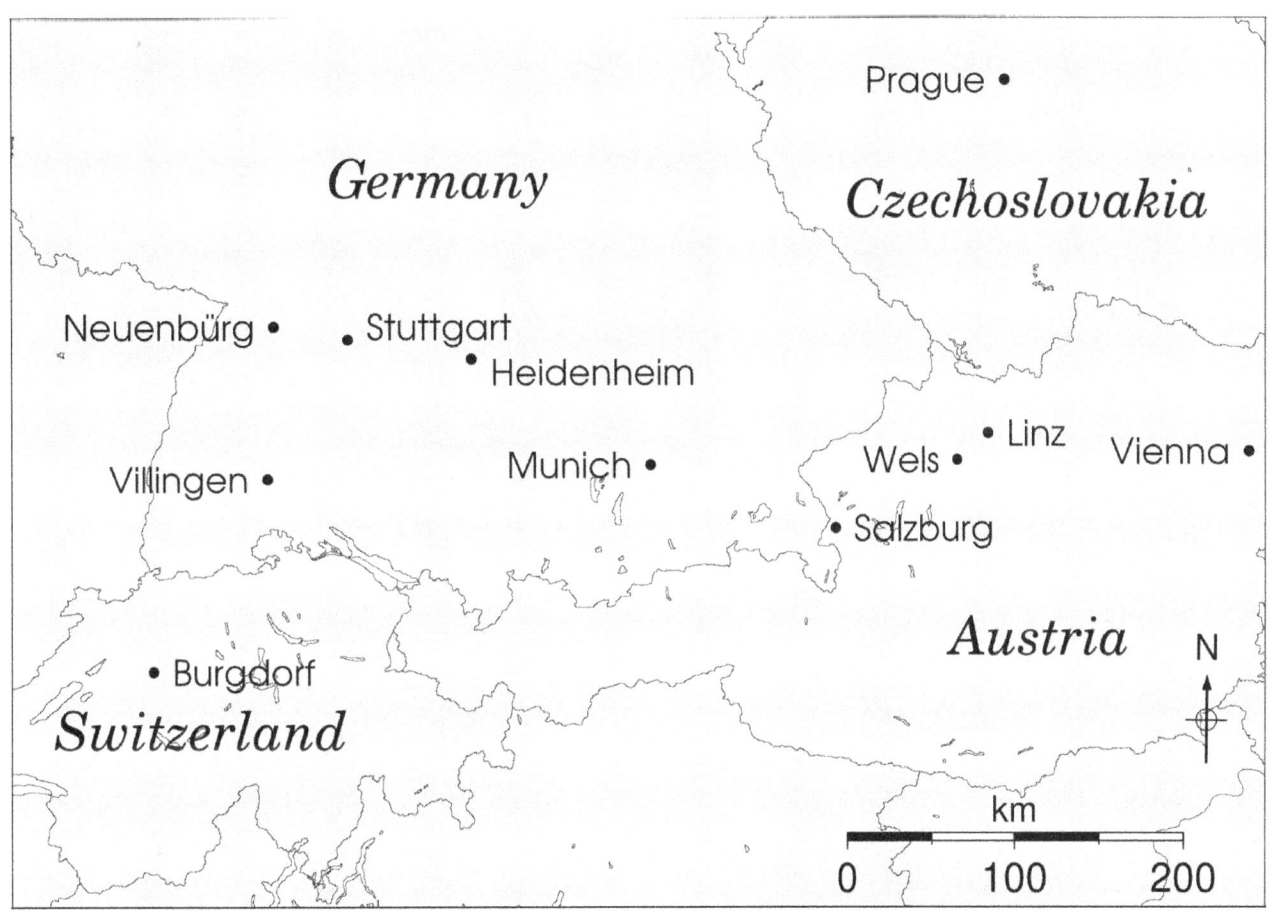

Map 3 Locations from Brigitte Kurowski-Wilson's time in Europe during and after the war

Appendix D: Illustrations and Photographs

1. My father at the window of his apartment in Heilbronn in 1911, with his sister Lydia.

2. My brothers Hans and Walter c. 1924, Honhardt.

3. My mother with Hans, Walter and me, in 1929 in front of the Honhardt schoolhouse.

4. My mother, Ilshofen, 1931.

5. My maternal grandmother, Ilshofen, 1931.

6. Standing in front of the entrance to the church yard in Sülzbach in 1931, age 6.

7. My father's self-portrait, 1935.

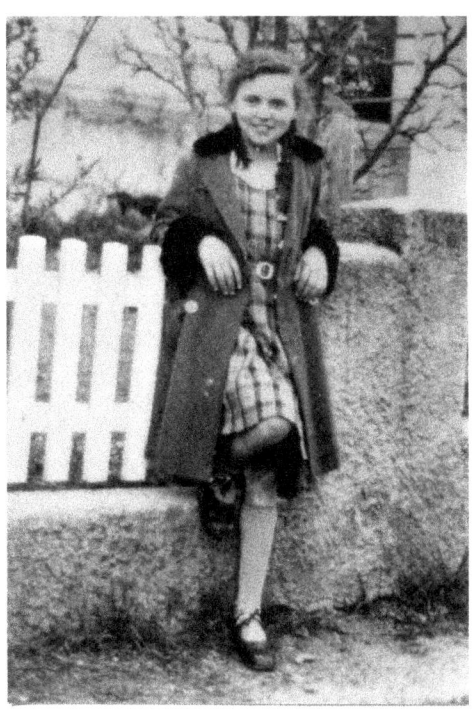

8. Öhringen, 1937.

9. My mother with my sister Liselotte in Öhringen, 1937, one year before my mother's death.

10. My brother Walter in 1938 in Ilshofen.

11. In my grandmother's garden in Ilshofen in 1940, age 16.

12. Putting on a play in boarding school in 1943 in Stuttgart; I am in the second row, second from the left.

13. Daily morning salute, Villa Berg in Stuttgart during the war, c. 1943.

14. In front of a canteen as a Red Cross nurse, winter 1945; I'm on the right.

15. My future husband Tadeusz in 1945 in Villingen, with a BMW sports car, after his liberation from the prisoner of war camp. He bought the car with 1000 cartons of cigarettes he had saved from Care parcels.

16. In Neuenbürg in 1948, standing on the right, next to a concentration camp survivor.

17. At the Swiss hosptial in Burgdorf, 1950.

18. Graduation from the school of nursing in Peterborough, 1956.

19. Graduation from the school of nursing in Peterborough, 1956.

20. My sister Liselotte in Ellhofen or Heilbronn, age approximately 28, c. 1963.

21. My brother Hans and his wife Majia, c. 1965.

22. My sister Liselotte's grave in Ellhofen in 1980.

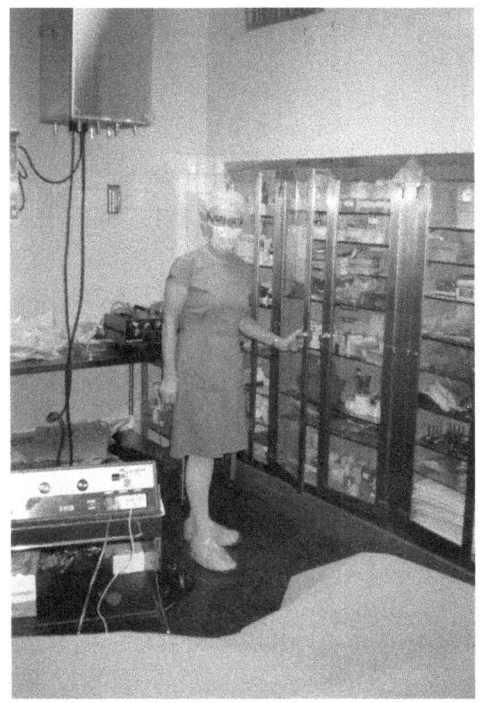

23. Operating room nurse at Peterborough Civic Hospital, 1989.

24. My sister Liselotte's three children in 2002 in Ellhofen.

25. In Nigeria in 2003, for the charity *Canadian Samaritans for Africa*.

26. With my nephew Hans-Peter and his wife Regina; as a birthday gift, they took me on a flight over the places I lived in central Europe; Schwäbisch Hall, 2005.

27. As a Eucharistic minister at the Cathedral Church of St. Peter-In-Chains in Peterborough, 2005.

28. With the medical brigade in Honduras, 2008.

www.ingramcontent.com/pod-product-compliance
Lightning Source LLC
Chambersburg PA
CBHW081458040426
42446CB00016B/3295